CW00631311

KIERKEGAARD AND NIETZSCHE

Also by J. Kellenberger

GOD-RELATIONSHIPS WITH AND WITHOUT GOD

INTER-RELIGIOUS MODELS AND CRITERIA (*editor*)

RELATIONSHIP MORALITY

RELIGIOUS DISCOVERY, FAITH AND KNOWLEDGE

THE COGNIVITY OF RELIGION: Three Perspectives

Kierkegaard and Nietzsche

Faith and Eternal Acceptance

J. Kellenberger
Professor of Philosophy
California State University
Northridge
California

First published in Great Britain 1997 by
MACMILLAN PRESS LTD
Houndmills, Basingstoke, Hampshire RG21 6XS and London
Companies and representatives throughout the world

This book is published in Macmillan's *Library of Philosophy and Religion*
Series
General editor: John Hick
Series ISBN 0–333–69996–3

A catalogue record for this book is available from the British Library.

ISBN 0–333–67656–4

 First published in the United States of America 1997 by
ST. MARTIN'S PRESS, INC.,
Scholarly and Reference Division,
175 Fifth Avenue, New York, N.Y. 10010

ISBN 0–312–17347–4

Library of Congress Cataloging-in-Publication Data
Kellenberger, James.
Kierkegaard and Nietzsche : faith and eternal acceptance / J.
Kellenberger
p.   cm.
Includes bibliographical references and index.
ISBN 0–312–17347–4 (cloth)
1. Kierkegaard, Søren, 1813–1855—Religion.   2. Nietzsche,
Friedrich Wilhelm, 1844–1900—Religion.   I. Title.
B4378.R44K45 1997
198'.9—dc21

96–46722
CIP

This book is printed on paper suitable for recycling and made from fully managed and
sustained forest sources.

10   9   8   7   6   5   4   3   2   1
06   05   04   03   02   01   00   99   98   97

Printed in Great Britain by
The Ipswich Book Company Ltd
Ipswich, Suffolk

To Anne

Contents

Preface

In the middle of the nineteenth century Matthew Arnold saw himself as 'Wandering between two worlds, one dead, / The other powerless to be born.' The world that was dead to Arnold was the world of faith. The new world struggling to be born was a world without faith. In the nineteenth century, against the background of urbanization, industrialization, scientific discovery, and expanding technology, the secularization of Europe, already some centuries old, continued to grow. It was not merely a social phenomenon. What Arnold refers to is a change, or a confrontation, in his deepest sensibilities.

Arnold, like many Victorians, cannot believe in God and is agitated by his lack of belief. The old world is dying or dead, and he mourns his loss of faith even while he recognizes that he cannot go back to the world of faith. At the same time he cannot bring into being the new world with its new meaning. He can but 'wander' between the two worlds.

The poem by Arnold from which these lines are taken, 'Stanzas from the Grande Chartreuse', was published in 1855, the year in which Søren Kierkegaard died and eleven years after the birth of Friedrich Nietzsche. Both Kierkegaard and Nietzsche were acutely aware of the dying of faith that invites Arnold's mournful sentiment. But, unlike Arnold, neither stands passively before it. Nietzsche, Matthew Arnold's later contemporary, does not mourn the passing of the old world, nor does he concede that the new world is powerless to be born; he exhorts his contemporaries to create the new world of value and meaning. Kierkegaard, Arnold's early contemporary, does not concede that the old world, the world of faith, is dead; rather, he sees his contemporaries as turning from the life-giving demands of the passion of faith, he sees his contemporaries as themselves dying away from faith; and he sets about making them aware of the true character of faith, so that they may reclaim it in their lives. In this way Kierkegaard and Nietzsche embody two active but opposite reactions to the dying of faith in Europe in the nineteenth century. However, these two authors speak to our own time, the twentieth and twenty-first centuries, as well; and though they are both Christian, or, in the case of

Nietzsche, of Christian background, both speak to other religious traditions that face the growing secularization of our sensibilities.

The nineteenth century has ended, but the social and religious phenomenon of secularization, in both its exterior and interior manifestations, continues. One hundred years later, at the end of the twentieth century and at the beginning of the twenty-first, beneath the brittle evolution of information technology and the general increase in the hubbub of life, this process is, if anything, growing in strength and influence. Now, though, it is not an exclusively European phenomenon. It is global, affecting all the religious traditions of the world. In this century Kierkegaard and Nietzsche are as relevant as they were in their century; in fact more so, for now their precocious voices are being heard in a way that they were never heard in their own time.

Each author offers to his and to our age a hope, a vision of acceptance of the world. But their visions are utterly different. Kierkegaard's flows from and is vivified by faith. Nietzsche's gains its sustenance from a rejection of the tradition of faith. This book is not an endeavour to canvas the full spectrum of Kierkegaard's thought, or of Nietzsche's, let alone the thought of both. It does, however, put into graphic and dialectical opposition two competing visions of joyful acceptance that we find in the works of these two thinkers – one profoundly religious, the other profoundly anti-religious – and it poses the question: Which vision of acceptance of life has, not only more relevance for us, but more truth?

Some material in Chapter 10 originally appeared as 'Three Models of Faith', *International Journal for the Philosophy of Religion*, vol. 12 (1981). Copyright © 1981 by Martinus Nijhoff Publishers, The Hague. Reprinted by permission of Kluwer Academic Publishers.

I am grateful for support in the form of reassigned time provided by the School of Humanities and the Department of Philosophy at California State University, Northridge. As in the past, the chair of the Philosophy Department, Daniel Sedey, aided my research and writing by giving me helpful teaching schedules. I also thank Annabelle Buckley for her editorial assistance and John M. Smith for his help in preparing the typescript for publication.

J. KELLENBERGER

Introduction

Kierkegaard and Nietzsche were autobiographical writers who never wrote an autobiography. It was not the explicit intention of either to write about himself. Nevertheless their written works came to express and to embody much of their lives, especially their inner lives. To be sure, the writings of any philosopher, like the novels of a writer of fiction, flow from and express the life-experience of the author. *In some way*, inevitably, what philosophers write reflects their experience – indirectly, if not directly, and perhaps as much in what they do not say as in what they do say. In at least this way the philosophical thinking of even the most formalistic analytic philosophers to a degree reflects their life-experiences. For other philosophers, more inclined towards psychological reflection, the degree to which their thinking reflects their experience is greater. Kierkegaard and Nietzsche were thinkers of the second sort, and at times their writings reflect in a fairly obvious way certain definite experiences in their lives. So it is that one can find in Kierkegaard's writings echoes of his romantic relationship to Regina Olsen and can find in Nietzsche's writings intimations of his relationship to Lou Salomé. Such echoes and intimations, however, are merely autobiographical snippets. In another, more significant, dimension the substance of what Kierkegaard and Nietzsche wrote about religion and value flows from and reflects their life-experiences. It is not too much to say that Kierkegaard and Nietzsche came to live in and through their writings. Thus it is Kierkegaard's own polyphonous voice that we hear in his pseudonymous works, when, for instance, he bodies forth the aesthetic, and it is Nietzsche's voice we hear in the prophecy of Zarathustra.

In this respect these authors, who are so radically different in the way they see life and the significance of life, are exactly similar. In other ways too, Kierkegaard and Nietzsche share a deep similarity. Both are psychologists – in the sense that Dostoyevsky was a psychologist. (Nietzsche, incidentally, said that Dostoyevsky was 'the only psychologist ... from whom I had something to learn.')[1] Like Dostoyevsky, each author explores the hidden feelings and motives that can shape a human life. Again, Kierkegaard and Nietzsche are profoundly similar in their absolute commitment to their writing,

1

to their 'work', to use Nietzsche's term.[2] Each lived a life of rigor-
ous solitude dedicated to his writing. Each was constantly writing:
Kierkegaard immured in his rooms in Copenhagen – the city he
never left except for an excursion within Denmark and several
visits to Berlin, Nietzsche in lodgings in the Engadin in Switzerland
or in northern Italy. During their intensely productive periods –
1843–50 for Kierkegaard and 1878–88 for Nietzsche – they turned
out a book a year, or, in the case of Kierkegaard, several books a
year. Kierkegaard would take walks and carriage rides for diversion. Nietzsche too took the air to restore himself before returning
for another bout of writing. In *Ecce Homo* Nietzsche tells us that all
of *Zarathustra* came to him in 1883 on his walks around the Gulf of
Rapello near Genoa.[3]

Another point of significant similarity: both are religious writers.
Both address the religion of their fathers. Their common heritage is
Christianity, but, moreover, they share Lutheran roots and upbringing. Both speak critically to the religion of their fathers, the
Christianity of their fathers. Nietzsche was the son of a Lutheran
minister and literally rejected his father's religion. Kierkegaard,
though he was never the pastor of a church, was qualified by theological training to be a pastor in the Lutheran Church of Denmark,
the established church of the state. Neither believes that religion
ultimately, as it expresses itself in the life of an individual, is
merely a matter of holding a set of significant religious propositions to be true. They agree that religion's subtler ramifications
require the probing of a psychologist. Each is concerned with the
connection between religious belief and ethics and between God
and morality.

Both are religious writers – but not just because their writings
share a religious target. Both authors can cite scripture and draw
sustenance from biblical themes. Both know Christian sensibility
from the inside. And each, out of his religious sensibility, speaks
critically to his religious tradition – although they do so in different
ways. Nietzsche challenges society to throw off the last vestiges of a
half-consciously rejected Christianity. Kierkegaard challenges the
society of 'Christendom' to become Christian. For Nietzsche, faith
falsifies human potential and vitiates the will to power. For
Kierkegaard, the members of Christendom affirm the doctrines of
Christianity, but lack faith. For Kierkegaard, the fault is in the established and socially accepted forms of religion, precisely because
they give no place to faith. For Nietzsche, the fault goes beyond the

established and socially accepted forms of religion and lies at the very heart of religion, and of Christianity in particular.

In one way Nietzsche, who proclaims the death of God, is more a religious writer than Kierkegaard. It is not Kierkegaard but Nietzsche who speaks as a prophet. Zarathustra, through whom Nietzsche speaks, is the prophet of the *Übermensch*.[4] As much as the prophets of the Old Testament, Zarathustra has a message to proclaim. However, he is not a prophet of the Lord. Thus saith the Lord, say Isaiah and Jeremiah. Thus spoke Zarathustra, says Nietzsche. Zarathustra speaks authoritatively, but on his own authority. Kierkegaard did not speak authoritatively – not as an apostle or as a prophet. In fact, in his pseudonymous works, he did not even speak 'directly', but 'indirectly'.

Yet both authors share the existential language of passion. Both understand that religion, when it enters into the life of an existing individual, *must* affect that individual's life through life-values that become internalized. For Nietzsche we are the slaves of a pervasive religious belief in God and must free ourselves of its baneful influence. For Kierkegaard, belief in God, religious faith in God, is something very different from the comfortable social belief of Christendom. For Nietzsche, God is dead and we have killed God, but we must bend our wills to accept our act, which, though our own act, is still distant from us. For Kierkegaard, faith is an entered God-relationship, filled with dread and joy, which is the highest passion a human being can attain, attainable by all, though – for all we can see – rarely attained. Kierkegaard and Nietzsche of course never met. Kierkegaard died in 1855, when Nietzsche was only eleven. But had they met as contemporaries they would have understood one another, they could have spoken to one another in a shared language.

A good part of the reason Kierkegaard and Nietzsche spoke the same language is that both probed beneath the surface of religion. Nietzsche accused religion of having hidden motives and springs: the secret motive of religion, or of Pauline Christianity at least, is revenge,[5] and belief in all gods is created by 'weariness [*Müdigkeit*]'.[6] Kierkegaard would have disagreed, but he would have felt the force of the claim and seen it as striking at the heart of religion in a way that the animadversions of Hume and the Enlightenment did not. Kierkegaard spoke out of a religious sensibility that would not have dismissed such a claim as irrelevant to what is essential to religious faith and commitment. Of course for

many what really counts in religion is, first, the truth of what is believed religiously and, second, the rational basis of religious belief.
This is the perspective of much traditional philosophy of religion,
going back to Hume, and much contemporary philosophy of religion done in the analytic tradition. Much analytic philosophy of religion is seemingly unaware of what both Nietzsche and
Kierkegaard are acutely aware of: that if the concern with doctrinal
truth and the concern with rationality have importance for the life
of religious faith, they do so by virtue of the psychological dimension of belief – the side of faith that analytic philosophy is inclined
to dismiss as irrelevant. I would argue, moreover, that in order to
approach a resolution of the concerns of truth and rationality that
does not violate a strain of religious sensibility deeply embedded in
Judaism and Christianity, one must heed the sorts of psychological
claims that animate the controversy between Kierkegaard and
Nietzsche. (I have argued this in an earlier book, *The Cognitivity of
Religion*.)[7] Our concern here, though, is a different one.

Here our concern is with joy, with the joyful acceptance of the
world. For Kierkegaard in *Fear and Trembling*, faith is joyful. A
joyful acceptance of the world is allied with faith as a fruit of the
spirit. Nietzsche, also, gives a central place to a joyful acceptance of
the world. But Nietzsche sees joyful acceptance as possible only
after the renunciation of all gods. At work here are very different
intuitions, correlated with deeply opposed worldviews and with
profoundly different conceptions of a fulfilled human life. A good
part of our enquiry will be to explore critically the different intuitions and background views of these two thinkers, this being a
necessary preliminary to the comparison of the joyful acceptance
projected by Kierkegaard with that projected by Nietzsche. A not
unimportant element of the opposition between Kierkegaard and
Nietzsche is the precise affective character of the joyful acceptance
that each proclaims. While in *Fear and Trembling* and in *Thus Spoke
Zarathustra* Kierkegaard and Nietzsche respectively project visions
of a fulfilled life that includes an enthusiastic – joyful – acceptance
of the world, this is not to say that the affective character of this acceptance is the same for both. For Kierkegaard in *Fear and Trembling*
joyful acceptance is a part of faith in God. For Nietzsche it flows
from a very different source. And, as we shall see, this difference
impinges on the subjective character of the acceptance of life.

In the first four chapters we shall examine the character of faith
and its joyful acceptance, as Kierkegaard presents them to us in

Fear and Trembling. Then, in the four chapters that follow, we shall bring forward Nietzsche's thinking, especially as it is spoken to us by Zarathustra. In Chapter 9, we shall compare the joyful acceptance that Kierkegaard finds in faith with Nietzsche's, and Zarathustra's, joyful acceptance of life. And, finally, in the last chapter we shall reflect on the ultimately irreconcilable point of opposition between Kierkegaard and Nietzsche and on how each of these two religious thinkers would have seen the other.

Part I

1

Abraham, the Knight of Faith

For Kierkegaard in the *Concluding Unscientific Postscript* it is 'the God-relationship that makes a human being a human being'.[1] By 'God-relationship' Kierkegaard does not mean the relationship that all persons have to God by virtue of being persons created by God. He means a faith-relationship, consciously entered and maintained. Faith in God, religious faith, for Kierkegaard, completes us as human beings and fulfils the potential our lives have for meaningfulness. In the Christendom of his day, he judged, faith had become confused with a habitual belief, acquired through the socially approved practice of the established church, completely convenient, and easily compatible with the serious pursuit of comfort. Kierkegaard's explicit concern is with the state of Christianity in his native Denmark; by extension, however, it would apply to the other nations of Christendom, and, indeed, to other religious traditions, including Judaism and Islam, where faith in God is central. Everywhere, Kierkegaard perceived, religion – faith – was being watered down, or 'levelled'. The essential paradox of faith, without which faith is not faith, had been or was being removed. On one front, the hard sayings of religion had been interpreted by accommodating exegetes so that no one would find anything offensive in them. On another front, faith, or what passed for faith, was being made quite reasonable by theological and philosophical apologists, who addressed the challenge to religion issued by the Enlightenment. Following such apologists, intellectual believers were prepared to 'go beyond' the faith of their fathers.

All of this Kierkegaard opposes. Faith is neither a comfortable belief nor something to go beyond: it is the highest attainment of an existing human being. Kierkegaard's effort in much of his authorship is to make clear the hard demands of faith – just the opposite of apologetics. In the *Postscript*, through the voice of the

9

pseudonymous Johannes Climacus, he says that in an age when modern inventions – he mentions steamships and the telegraph – are making life easier and easier he wants 'to make something more difficult'.[2] He wants to make faith 'more difficult' – but no more difficult than it really is.[3]

Kierkegaard pursues this theme in more than one work. The Kierkegaardian work that we shall focus on in this enquiry is *Fear and Trembling*, for Kierkegaard's thinking in this work has implications for the character and source of joyful acceptance that (as we shall see) address the thinking of Nietzsche. In *Fear and Trembling* the exemplar of faith is Abraham, the paradigmatic 'knight of faith', and the pseudonymous author of *Fear and Trembling* endeavours to show us what faith is through a dialectical reflection on Abraham's character and manner of action in his trial of faith.

The pseudonymous author of *Fear and Trembling* is not Johannes Climacus, but Johannes de Silentio. Before I proceed further perhaps I should say a word about Kierkegaard's pseudonyms and how I shall treat them. Kierkegaard left a pseudonymous corpus, consisting of a number of works authored by a variety of pseudonymous authors. As Johannes Climacus is the author of *Philosophical Fragments* and the *Concluding Unscientific Postscript*, so Johannes de Silentio is the author of *Fear and Trembling* and Anti-Climacus is the author of *The Sickness unto Death*, and so on. Kierkegaard presses into duty more than ten pseudonymous authors. Often the works by these authors share themes and even special categories. The four works just mentioned share Kierkegaard's central concern with faith, although *The Sickness unto Death* is more concerned with the forms of the failure to have faith (the forms of despair) than with the demands of faith. *Fear and Trembling* by Johannes de Silentio and the *Postscript* by Johannes Climacus are more closely aligned in that they share a concern with the demands of faith: both pseudonymous authors want to force comfortable believers to confront the hard demands of faith. I intend to respect Kierkegaard's use of pseudonyms. At the end of the *Postscript*, speaking in his own voice in an addendum, Kierkegaard says that 'in the pseudonymous books there is not a single word by me' and that he is 'just as little' one pseudonymous author as another.[4] Kierkegaard, then, is a polyphonous author with many voices, and in the choir of his pseudonymous author-ship each voice speaks with its own internal integrity. As a consequence it is wrong or dangerous glibly to quote a work by one

pseudonymous author in order to interpret a different pseudonymous work by a different pseudonymous author. It is wrong to
assume that we can always quote Johannes Climacus to clarify
what Johannes de Silentio meant. And this is so even though both
authors are addressing the same concern – the demands of faith –
for they project different constructions of faith; and they do so even
though both authors share categories (such as the absurd) for they
may not understand their categories in the same way. I do not
mean that we can never draw upon one work to amplify what is
said in another – something I have already done. However, we
must do this circumspectly and not assume that whatever one
pseudonymous author says will be compatible with whatever
another pseudonymous author says.

In *Fear and Trembling*, as I say, Johannes de Silentio bodies forth
faith and its hard demands by means of a narrative of an exemplar
of faith: Abraham. In the *Postscript* Climacus proceeds very differ-
ently: he provides a definition of faith, the famous *Postscript*
definition of '[subjective] truth', which he says is also a definition of
faith.[5] Johannes de Silentio never defines faith. This is not an unimportant difference between the two pseudonymous authors. Also,
and even more importantly, the two authors give us two different
and opposed models of faith. Given our concerns, this is not the
place to dwell upon the details of the *Postscript* model and why it is
different from the *Fear and Trembling* model. Suffice it to say that for
Climacus in the *Postscript* faith is a continuing struggle to overcome
one's doubts and hold fast to belief in an 'objective uncertainty',
while for Johannes de Silentio in *Fear and Trembling* doubt is a
failure of faith and the knight of faith does not doubt (and so does
not struggle with his/her doubt) but sees as certain what he/she
holds fast in belief: in the *Postscript*, we may say, the cry of faith is,
'It cannot be, all reason is against it; yet I believe!' while in *Fear and
Trembling* the cry of faith that fits Abraham's faith is, 'I know that
God's promise is true!' (in perfect analogy with Job's expression of
his faith, 'I know that my Redeemer lives' (Job 19:25)).[6] There are
further related differences between these models, although there
are significant similarities as well. For both Johannes de Silentio
and Climacus, faith is not a comfortable social or habitual belief;
for both, faith is a passion – and faith is a God-relationship. Thus, at
times, if we exercise care, we may be able to draw upon Climacus'
reflections to amplify points brought forward by Johannes de
Silentio.

Now let us resume our discussion of *Fear and Trembling*. In that work Johannes de Silentio tries to bring out what faith demands by presenting and reflecting on Abraham in his trial of faith. He tells, or retells, the story of Abraham and Isaac, and turns it this way and that to bring out the character of Abraham's faith. But just as he does not venture a definition of faith, so Johannes does not proclaim what faith is. Johannes uses 'indirect communication': he, by his own confession, cannot directly tell us what faith is, and so what it demands, but he can tell us indirectly. What this distinction comes to, in *Fear and Trembling* at least, is indicated by the book's epigraph: 'What Tarquinius Superbus said in the garden by means of the poppies, the son understood but the messenger did not.'[7] In the episode alluded to, when the son of Tarquinius Superbus had gained control of a city he sent a messenger to his father for instructions; Tarquinius made no reply to the messenger but took him into the garden and with his cane struck off the heads of the tallest poppies. When the messenger returned and recounted what Tarquinius did the son understood that he must execute the leaders of the city. In this way the messenger conveyed a message from the father to his son without understanding the message or even that what he recounted conveyed a message. In a similar way Johannes de Silentio will convey what faith is, though he himself is not able to understand the significance of what he conveys. He must be 'silent', for he cannot understand faith. He stands in awe before Abraham's faith and cannot comprehend it. But, though he cannot directly state what faith is, Johannes can indirectly communicate the nature and demands of faith, which he does by describing and celebrating Abraham through retelling the story of Abraham's trial of faith, and by dialectically elaborating the demands of faith through contrasting Abraham's faith with what it is not.

The story that Johannes retells is the Genesis story of Abraham's trial of faith in which God tests his faith (Gen. 22:1–13).[8] It fits into a larger biblical story of Abraham and Isaac (in Gen. 17 and 22), which sets the stage for *Fear and Trembling*. The larger story, paraphrased, is this:

> God appears before Abraham when he is 99 years old and tells him that he shall be the father of a multitude of nations. God announces that Abraham's wife Sarah shall have a son, to be called Isaac, and God promises that His covenant with Abraham shall also be established with the descendants of Isaac. Then, after

some years, God tests Abraham. He tells Abraham to take his only son Isaac, whom he loves, to the land of Moriah and there to prepare Isaac as a sacrifice. Abraham arises early in the morning and does as the Lord commands. He takes Isaac to Moriah, prepares the altar for a burnt offering, and binds Isaac. Then the angel of the Lord shows him a ram caught in a thicket. Abraham sacrifices the ram, and he and Isaac return home.

The part of this larger story that Johannes uses to bring out the character of Abraham's faith is the part in which Abraham responds to God's command to take Isaac to Moriah and there to sacrifice him. However, the first part of the larger story is importantly in the background of Johannes' treatment in *Fear and Trembling*. Johannes uses the story of Abraham's trial to bring out the nature and the demands of faith, as they are embodied in the story. His concern, then, is an internal concern with what the story conveys. It is not the external concern with whether the story is true. He never raises this question – nor need he, given his internal concern. Nor does he draw upon any of the other biblical stories involving Abraham, such as that in which Abraham contends with God over sparing Sodom (Gen. 18:22–33) or that in which Abraham (while still Abram) obtains the blessing of Melchizedek, the priest of God Most High (Gen. 14:18–20) – save for one passing mention of the first.[9] The faith of Abraham that Johannes would make palpable is the faith Abraham exhibits in the crisis of God's test.

What is the character of Abraham's faith, as Johannes de Silentio elicits it from the biblical narrative? For Johannes, in his retelling,[10] Abraham, as in the biblical account, arises early on the day that he and Isaac are to begin their journey to the land of Moriah. Abraham loves Isaac, but he does as God commands. He does not hang back, nor does he rush forward. For several days they journey toward Mount Moriah. When they arrive, Abraham cuts the wood, prepares the altar, and binds Isaac. In all of this he acts out of his faith, and he does not waver.[11]

Nor does he doubt. If Abraham had doubted, Johannes says, then he would have been remembered – but not for his faith.[12]

What is it that Abraham does not doubt? It is precisely that Isaac will not be demanded of him.[13] As Abraham travels to Moriah, fully intending to do as God has commanded, he has no doubt that Isaac will live! In Johannes' retelling, not doubting is a *sine qua non* of Abraham's faith. And, we should note, *what* is not doubted is a definite proposition: 'Isaac will not be lost to me; he will live.' This proposition is the direct object of Abraham's faith, as we may put it.

What Abraham believes, Johannes wants us to recognize, is not that he, Abraham, will be given a second Isaac in some future life. Abraham's faith is for this life. His faith is that Isaac, his son, the very son who is accompanying him on his journey to Moriah, will live.[14]

And Abraham has unwavering faith that this will be so even as he raises the sacrificial knife. More than this, Johannes reflects, Abraham must believe and not doubt that Isaac will not be lost to him even though he should bring down the knife.[15]

So, what Abraham must believe is 'preposterous' – nevertheless he does not doubt.[16] He has faith 'by virtue of the absurd', Johannes de Silentio tells us.[17] Just here, then, the *Fear and Trembling* category of the absurd emerges. What Johannes means by 'the absurd' is that which is beyond 'human calculation'.[18] The absurd is that which is beyond and counter to human common sense – as it is counter to common sense that Abraham can do as God commanded and yet Isaac will live. Abraham, as a knight of faith, believes, and acts, by virtue of the absurd.[19]

Yet, though he believes and though he acts resolutely, Abraham is in anxiety. 'What is omitted from Abraham's story is the anxiety', says Johannes de Silentio.[20] And he makes certain to include Abraham's anxiety in his own retelling. In fact, for Johannes, it would be impossible to tell Abraham's story leaving out the anxiety, for anxiety is an essential constituent of his faith. There are several reasons why Abraham is in anxiety. Let us note three. For one thing, Abraham is acting against the ethical. As Johannes puts it, 'The ethical expression for what Abraham did is that he meant to murder Isaac.'[21] Second, since Abraham acts by virtue of the absurd, he cannot communicate or explain his actions, and so is outside the understanding of others. Third, the physical nature of what he must undertake – preparing his son for sacrifice – is itself dread-producing.

Though in anxiety throughout his trial, Abraham acts resolutely and has no doubt that Isaac will live. It should be observed that for Johannes de Silentio anxiety is not doubt. Anxiety is a part of faith. Doubt is a failure of faith. Doubt opposes and rules out faith. For the *Fear and Trembling* model of faith, then, doubt, but not anxiety, is a form of despair, despair being the lack of faith. (That despair and faith are related as opposites is a point agreed upon throughout the pseudonymous corpus.) Abraham must experience dread, but he cannot doubt. Johannes de Silentio's implicit psychological point that one can experience an anxiety that does not presuppose doubt seems to me to be exactly right. However, in case the point's correctness is not immediately clear, let me say a word about it. First, we should appreciate, Johannes is not denying that we can be anxious because things are doubtful, as when we are anxious about what may or may not happen in the future. But, his point affirms, we can be anxious about, feel dread before, what does not involve our doubt or uncertainty. For instance, if I may provide an example or two, one may feel dread handling a gun even when one fully appreciates that it is unloaded, or again, one may feel anxious when asked to hold a realistic rubber spider though one is certain that it is not a real spider. Horror stories and films, if successful, will elicit a sense of dread, but the source of dread is not doubt regarding whether some horrific being might be threatening us or even exists. We may know perfectly well that there is no such being – and feel dread nevertheless. Accordingly, Johannes is correct in his portrait of Abraham: Abraham can at once have no doubt that Isaac will live and proceed in anxiety to carry out God's command, his anxiety having its source, not in his doubt about what will happen to Isaac, but in the three reasons for his anxiety that I have identified.

The year following the publication of *Fear and Trembling* Kierkegaard published *The Concept of Anxiety [Dread] (Begrebet Angest)*. In it anxiety is compared with dizziness by the pseudonymous author Virgilius Haufniensis: 'anxiety is the dizziness of freedom', he says.[22] For Haufniensis, anxiety always relates to the future and its open possibility.[23] Moreover it is both the presupposition of hereditary sin and the consequence of sin.[24] For Haufniensis, the relationship between faith and anxiety is that faith alone can 'renounce anxiety without anxiety', by which faith 'extricates itself from the moment of death'.[25] Clearly, this is not precisely the understanding of anxiety we find in *Fear and Trembling*. For one thing, for Johannes de Silentio, anxiety is not connected to sin as it is for Haufniensis – Abraham's anxiety does not flow from or lead to sin. For another thing, Johannes regards anxiety as a constituent of faith, not a separate condition from which faith must free

AB has doubt in the sense that he has no rational ground for his faith. Isn't this what we usually mean by doubt.

In this case my argument would be the same.

itself. This divergence of understanding is tolerable, given that the two works have different pseudonymous authors. Yet, to a significant degree, the two constructions of anxiety are in accord. When Virgilius Haufniensis says that anxiety is the dizziness of freedom and connects it to the open possibilities of the future, he does not, or need not, deny Johannes de Silentio's point that doubt and anxiety are distinguishable and not necessarily concomitants. Virgilius Haufniensis does not consider Abraham, but if he had he would have located his anxiety in his freedom either to do as God commands or not to do as God commands, the two possibilities open to him. Even if this is right, observe, it is not ruled out that Abraham has no doubt that Isaac will live whatever he does, for it remains that God has promised as much.

In any case, in *Fear and Trembling* Abraham does what is dreadful, and he *feels* the dread, he proceeds in fear and trembling – but he does not doubt that Isaac will not be lost to him. That Isaac will not be lost to him is the direct object of Abraham's faith, as I have put it. However, faith, for Johannes de Silentio, is not a relationship to a proposition, it is a relationship to God. Faith is a God-relationship (to use the *Postscript* term), an 'absolute relation to the absolute', as Johannes de Silentio puts it.[26] Faith in *Fear and Trembling* – and not in *Fear and Trembling* alone, of course – relates to trust in God. If Abraham does not obey God, his individual relationship to God will be violated, and Abraham will sin against God through his disobedience. But also Abraham's individual and absolute relationship to God is a faith relationship. It is the relationship of faith *in* God, and faith in God is, or essentially involves, trust in God. Thus, since his faith relationship to God requires trust, Abraham will violate his faith relationship if he fails to trust in God. And now we can see why he must believe that Isaac will not die, why this direct object of his faith is essential to his faith in God, his faith relationship to God. If he fails to believe that Isaac will live, then he will no longer believe that through Isaac he will be the father of a multitude of nations and that Isaac's descendants will participate in the covenant that God has established. But God had promised these things. God had promised that *through Isaac* Abraham will be the father of nations and that *through Isaac* Isaac's descendants will be established in His covenant. So it is that in order to believe that God will keep His promise Abraham must believe that Isaac will live. And so it is that if Abraham doubts that Isaac will live, then, by this, he would doubt that God will keep His promise – and in so

But this reintroduces the ethical as I's meaning

doing he would fail in his trust and so in his faith in God, and by this failure of trust violate his faith relationship to God. Abraham is the paradigmatic knight of faith, not because he believed that Isaac will live as an isolated item of faith, but because in his trial of faith he continued unwaveringly to trust in God, which he could do only by believing with utter conviction that Isaac will not be demanded of him.

Fear and Trembling is subtitled a 'Dialectical Lyric': on the one hand Johannes de Silentio throughout the work lyrically praises and expresses his awe before Abraham's prodigious faith; on the other hand, early and late, he dialectically contrasts Abraham's faith with what it is not. Early on, in the 'Exordium' or prelude, he provides four contrasting pictures of Abraham. Each is a picture of an Abraham without faith, an Abraham who is not Abraham.[27] A brief examination of each of the four is worthwhile.

The first picture: Abraham takes Isaac to Moriah, as he was commanded. When Isaac begs for his life, this Abraham tries to take the blame on himself. 'I am not your father', he tells Isaac, 'I am an idolator.' For, he reasons, it is better that Isaac should go out of this world believing his father a monster than that Isaac should lose his faith in God. This Abraham, we cannot but feel, is generous, even magnanimous in his self-abnegation, for he renounces the love Isaac has for him for the sake of Isaac. But this Abraham has ceased to see God as good. He has ceased to trust in God. On his own initiative he intercedes to correct the evil that God has allowed.

The second picture: Abraham does as he is commanded, but he is resigned to losing Isaac. He does what he is commanded to do, but silently and in resignation. He believes Isaac will be lost to him and he accepts the loss of his son. This Abraham cannot believe what faith requires. When all is over and he returns home with Isaac after sacrificing the ram provided by God, his 'eyes were darkened, and he saw joy no more'.

The third picture: Abraham sees his willingness to sacrifice Isaac as a sin. This Abraham sees things ethically, and the ethical expression for what Abraham did, Johannes de Silentio tells us, is that he meant to murder Isaac. This Abraham cannot believe God's command is good, for it goes counter to the ethical. This Abraham would sacrifice himself in place of Isaac, but he cannot believe that it will be forgiven that he was willing to sacrifice Isaac, his own son.

The fourth picture: Abraham does as he is commanded. Without undue haste he proceeds to Mount Moriah with Isaac. Calmly he makes things ready for the sacrifice. When he draws the knife, however, his left hand is 'clenched in despair' and a 'shudder' goes through his body. After the ram has been sacrificed they return home – but Isaac has lost his faith. In *Fear and Trembling* despair, of course, is the opposite of faith and rules out faith. Thus Johannes de Silentio in telling us that Abraham's hand is clenched in despair in effect tells us that Abraham has lost his faith. This Abraham is not the father of faith and has no faith with which to inspire his son, who, accordingly, loses his faith. The 'shudder' that goes through Abraham's body we may understand as a shudder of doubt, which in *Fear and Trembling* entails a failure of faith and so despair. The shudder that this Abraham experiences, then, is not the trembling of fear and trembling. The Danish word used by Kierkegaard, which translates as 'shudder', is *Skjælven*: the same word used in James 2:19, 'Even the demons believe – and shudder' The Danish word for 'trembling', used in the title *Fear and Trembling*, is *Bæven*: the Psalmist says to 'serve the Lord with fear and rejoice with trembling' (Psalm 2:11) and Paul says to 'work out your own salvation in fear and trembling' (Phil. 2:12).

In each of these four pictures of a possible Abraham, Johannes de Silentio graphically presents an Abraham with a very human response that we can understand, sympathize with, and even admire. However, each response is a simulacrum of faith. Abraham's faith, unlike these responses, is not open to our understanding. Johannes can only stand in awe before Abraham's faith. Johannes, then, in the Exordium helps to bring into relief the full demands of faith by contrasting Abraham's faith with what it is not, even though he cannot directly tell us what faith is and demands. For Johannes, faith of course contrasts with social or habitual belief, but also it contrasts with these more passionately engaged human responses.

What we have seen thus far is the character of Abraham's faith, as it emerges in Johannes' retelling of the story of Abraham's trial, and how Abraham's faith dialectically contrasts with four simulacra of faith. There is more to the dialectical movement of *Fear and Trembling*, which we shall explore later (in Chapter 3), but we have seen enough to appreciate the essential character of the *Fear and Trembling* model of faith. The faith Abraham exhibits in his trial, we should appreciate, is tested but not created by his trial. Abraham had faith and was the paradigmatic knight of faith before his trial of faith. This means that, before he was tested by God, he did not doubt, he was in anxiety, and he believed and acted by virtue of the absurd. A knight of faith, Johannes de Silentio tells us, 'does not do even the slightest thing except by virtue of the absurd'.[28] Abraham before his trial, while happy with Sarah and Isaac and content with the prosperity he enjoyed, even then, believed and acted only by virtue of the absurd.

Finally, before we conclude this chapter, there is one other crucial element of Abraham's faith that we should consider: Abraham's joy. This element is crucial to the rendering of faith in *Fear and Trembling* in that, for Johannes, if joy is lacking, faith is lacking. Thus the contrast between Abraham, the knight of faith, and the Abraham in the second picture of the Exordium, who 'saw joy no more'. Also it is crucial to our general purpose in this enquiry, which is to compare the joyful acceptance of faith with Zarathustra's joyful acceptance. Faith, for Kierkegaard, is a paradox. As Johannes de Silentio expresses it, 'faith is precisely the paradox that the single individual is higher than the universal [the ethical]'.[29] But also faith is paradoxical in that it is essentially joyful: Abraham, even in his trial, even in his anxiety, is joyful! The passion of faith – and faith is a passion for Johannes[30] – is importantly trust, trust in the presence of anxiety, and it is joy, joy found by virtue of the absurd.[31] I have tried to show how Abraham, as the knight of faith, can have anxiety while not doubting. But how can he be joyful, not only before but during his trial of faith? As the knight of faith, Abraham must be joyful. But how can he be? Why Abraham is joyful we take up in the next chapter.

2

The Joyfulness of Faith

Abraham finds joy by virtue of the absurd, Johannes de Silentio tells us. Abraham believes and acts by virtue of the absurd – and he finds joy by virtue of the absurd. Whence this joy? If it is gained by virtue of the absurd, is it going to be beyond our understanding and thus, for all we can tell, simply gratuitous, an arbitrary adornment to Johannes' portrait of Abraham? No, I suggest that Abraham's joy is in a way we can understand integral to his faith and his trust in God. In fact if he were not joyful, his faith and trust would be lacking.

Why is Abraham joyful? He is joyful for the same reason that he does not doubt that Isaac will live: Abraham *knows* that he will not lose Isaac. Though he proceeds in fear and trembling, and in anxiety, he is joyfully confident that Isaac, the son he loves, will not be taken from him. In the story of Abraham and Isaac, as Johannes de Silentio retells it, Abraham has no doubt. Indeed, in *Fear and Trembling* it is a condition of Abraham's faith that he not doubt. His not doubting that Isaac will live means that he is certain that Isaac will live. If he is certain, then, at least in his own eyes, he *knows* that Isaac will live. Being certain, of course, is not sufficient for having knowledge, but it is sufficient for one's seeing oneself as knowing. In the story, as Johannes de Silentio retells it, Abraham, being certain, must see himself as knowing. And within the story he *does* know, for it is a part of the story that God himself has promised Abraham that Isaac will not be lost to him.

Here, in *Fear and Trembling*, faith and knowledge go together. To experience doubt is at once to suffer a failure of faith and to exclude knowledge. Abraham is joyful because he knows that, despite the test he must endure, all will be well and Isaac will not be taken from him. For the model of faith we find in *Fear and Trembling* the confidence of Abraham's knowledge is an expression of his faith. This is a biblical model of faith. As I said earlier, it animates Job's cry of faith, 'I know that my Redeemer lives.' And it is this model of faith that pertains when Peter is rebuked by Jesus, 'O man of little faith, why did you doubt?' Peter is bid by Jesus to walk to him across the water. Peter does so; however, when he becomes afraid he begins to sink. Jesus reaches out his hand and saves him, but also he rebukes Peter for his failure of faith (Mt. 14:28–31). When Peter doubts that he can do as Jesus bids him do, he exhibits his lack of faith that he can do as Jesus bids (this proposition being, in that situation, the direct object of his faith), and in the same instant he shows his lack of faith in Jesus, which is to say his lack of trust in Jesus. In the story of Job, and in this story of Peter, the model of faith is such that in order to have faith one must have no doubt, and if one proclaims that one knows, one expresses thereby one's faith and one's trust. So Johannes presents Abraham's faith in *Fear and Trembling*, although the connection between faith and knowledge posited by the *Fear and Trembling* model is left implicit by Johannes. Johannes never says, nor does he deny, that Abraham knows that Isaac will live. He does say that Abraham knew it was God who was testing him.[1] However, that God is testing him is not the object of Abraham's faith in his trial of faith. What Abraham must not doubt, and must be prepared to proclaim he knows, is that Isaac will live – though he bring down the knife.

The *Fear and Trembling* model of faith, as we have seen, is at odds with the *Postscript* model, where faith is the struggle to believe in the face of uncertainty. Since, for Climacus, faith requires a struggle to overcome one's own doubts in the face of what one sees as uncertain, it is not surprising that Climacus explicitly opposes faith, or belief, and knowing.[2] Johannes de Silentio, though, never pronounces an opposition between faith and knowledge. The *Postscript* idea that faith opposes knowledge and requires doubt to struggle against expresses, it seems to me, certain discernible religious sensibilities, just as the *Fear and Trembling* model does. Moreover, the *Postscript* model also gains nourishment from at least one biblical story. I have in mind the story of the father who begs Jesus to heal his son, apparently an epileptic, who is seized by convulsions (Mk 9:20–25). 'All things are possible to him who believes', Jesus tells the father. The father immediately cries out, 'I believe, help my unbelief.' That Jesus then cures the boy provides a sanction of this instance of faith struggling with uncertainty.

The *Postscript* model may also be interpreted as agreeing with the definition of faith in The Letter to the Hebrews, where we are told that 'faith is the assurance of things hoped for, the conviction of things not seen' (Heb. 11:1). The *Postscript* model agrees with this definition if we read 'assurance' and 'conviction', not as 'certainty', but as 'strong commitment of belief' and read 'not seen' as 'not known to the one with faith'. But the *Fear and Trembling* model does just as well, even better here. It agrees with the definition in Hebrews if we read 'assurance' and 'conviction' straightforwardly as 'certainty' and read 'not seen' as 'not known to the world at large' or 'not seen with the eyes of flesh', that is, not visually or empirically seen (which is what Jesus means by 'not seen' when he tells Thomas, 'Blessed are those who have not seen and yet believe' (Jn 20:29)).

In any case, whatever the relation of the *Fear and Trembling* model to the *Postscript* model or to the definition of faith in Hebrews, for Johannes de Silentio, faith requires certainty, and faith and knowledge go together. Abraham believes and acts by virtue of the absurd, for Johannes. Also, we may add, going beyond what Johannes explicitly says, in *Fear and Trembling* Abraham *knows* by virtue of the absurd. Let me say why this is so. Abraham can answer the question 'How do you know that Isaac will live?' He can reply: 'God has promised that Isaac will live, for He has promised that through Isaac I shall be the father of nations and that through Isaac his descendants will share in the covenant, and so I know that God will not demand Isaac even though He has commanded me to sacrifice him.' But that Isaac will live though Abraham should carry out God's command goes against all that we understand: it goes against common sense. This is to say that it is absurd in the *Fear and Trembling* sense of 'absurd'. Abraham, then, can say why he believes and even how he knows, but what he says does not explain. The words he utters do not constitute an explanation of how he knows, for they do not amount to an explanation that others can understand. What he says, or would say, is absurd.

Nevertheless, within the story, Abraham does know that Isaac will live – even though how he knows is by virtue of something that does not explain his knowing to others. And he is joyful because he knows.

Abraham, then, we should imagine as joyfully giving thanks to God *in* his trial of faith. His biblical faith is quite in accord with the Psalmist's feeling when he says: 'I will bless the Lord at all times; his praise shall continually be in my mouth' (Ps. 34:1). And it is in accord with what Paul writes to the Thessalonians: 'Rejoice always, pray constantly, give thanks in all circumstances' (1 Thess. 5:16–18). Abraham has, integral to his faith, that joy which is a fruit of the Spirit (Gal. 5:22), attained by virtue of the absurd for Johannes in *Fear and Trembling*, and, at the same time, gained by Abraham through his knowledge that God in His goodness will not demand Isaac. Abraham knows by virtue of the absurd, and he is joyful and rejoices because he has the confidence of his knowledge.

Abraham knows that he will not lose Isaac, and he knows that he will not because he has God's promise. Because he knows that all will be well and he will not lose Isaac, he is joyful and rejoices in what he has been given. We should be careful, however, to keep our focus on just what, in *Fear and Trembling*, Abraham knows that yields his joy. It is the direct object of his faith, that Isaac will live, that precise preposterous proposition. It is not any of the other things that, in the story Johannes de Silentio retells, Abraham knew. That Abraham knew it was God who made the promise is given in the story, and it is given in the story that Abraham knew it was God who was testing him. The trial of Abraham's faith does not relate to these elements of the story but comes after they are in place. Throughout *Fear and Trembling* Johannes de Silentio is steadily clear that the direct object of Abraham's faith in his trial of faith is that he, Abraham, will not lose Isaac. The direct object of Abraham's faith for Johannes, we should be clear, is not that there is a God or that it was God who gave him the promise or that it was God who gave him the command to take Isaac to Mount Moriah. The direct object of Abraham's faith in his trial is that the God who made the promise and who commanded him to sacrifice Isaac will nevertheless not demand Isaac of him.

There is room for confusion on this and related points, and it seems to me that one who did not have Kierkegaard, or Johannes de Silentio, quite right here is Jean-Paul Sartre. Sartre wrote in *Existentialism*:

> Anguish is evident even when it conceals itself. This is the anguish that Kierkegaard called the anguish of Abraham. You know the story: an angel has ordered Abraham to sacrifice his son; if it really were an angel who has come and said, 'You are Abraham, you shall sacrifice your son,' everything would be all right. But everyone might first wonder, 'Is it really an angel, and am I really Abraham? What proof do I have?'[3]

And, Sartre goes on to say, 'If a voice addresses me, it is always for me to decide that this is the angel's voice.'[4]

Sartre is thinking of anguish as arising from the 'freedom' Abraham faces. In *Being and Nothingness* Sartre agrees with Kierkegaard that anguish is 'anguish in the face of freedom'.[5] Clearly, in this reading of Kierkegaard Sartre is drawing upon *The Concept of Anxiety* by the pseudonymous Virgilius Haufniensis. In that work, as we have seen, anxiety is 'the dizziness of freedom'. So, on this specific point Kierkegaard, or rather Virgilius Haufniensis, and Sartre can agree. But in the quoted passage from *Existentialism* Sartre goes on to apply this understanding of anxiety to Kierkegaard's Abraham – which is to say to the Abraham of *Fear and Trembling* – and, more-over, to apply it along with his own set of assumptions.

For one thing, Sartre has Abraham's anguish deriving from his not being certain, and so having to 'decide' whether it is an angel's voice he hears. But in *Fear and Trembling*, as I have argued, Abraham's anxiety does not arise from any uncertainty that he has. He is certain that Isaac will live. Interestingly, Sartre does not iden-tify this proposition as a proposition in need of 'proof'; he identifies two others. Thus he leaves out entirely the direct object of Abraham's faith in *Fear and Trembling*. Sartre imagines Abraham to be dubious about, first, whether he is really Abraham, and, second, whether it is really an angel – that is, really God – who is ordering him to sacrifice his son. However, Abraham, as Johannes de Silentio presents him, does not doubt or feel he needs 'proof' for either of Sartre's two propositions. In *Fear and Trembling* Abraham does not doubt or feel he needs 'proof' that he is Abraham. In the background story in Genesis when God tests Abraham He calls to him, 'Abraham', and Abraham responds, 'Here am I' (Gen. 22:1). Nor does Abraham doubt that it is God who commands him. These are things Abraham knows as a part of the background story. To be sure, Johannes de Silentio does not tell us *how* Abraham knew that it was God who was testing him – just as he does not tell us *how* Abraham knew that it was God who promised him that through Isaac he would be the father of nations and that through Isaac his and Isaac's descendants would partici-pate in the covenant. It is simply part of the background story, assumed by Johannes de Silentio, that Abraham knows these things.

Sartre, and others too, may 'wonder' and ask questions about how Abraham knew these things and about their truth – but Sartre has *Fear and Trembling* wrong when he attributes uncertainty about them to Johannes de Silentio's Abraham. Sartre can of course give his own interpretation of Abraham's story, one in which Abraham has these Sartrian questions, but such an interpretation would be Sartre's retelling of the story, not that of Johannes de Silentio, and Sartre's Abraham would not be a knight of faith.

For Johannes de Silentio, Abraham knows that there is a God, that God promised him what He did, and that it was God who was testing him. But also, and more significantly, given Abraham's particular trial of faith, Abraham knows that Isaac will live. Further, Abraham knows this in the midst of his anxiety. Sartre is right about this much: Abraham, the Abraham of *Fear and Trembling*, is in anxiety. In the last chapter I identified three sources of Abraham's anxiety: (1) Abraham's relation to the ethical, (2) the absence of understanding from others, and (3) the nature of the act he was called upon to perform. Abraham's anxiety, then, I argued, should not be attributed to any uncertainty he has about what he is called upon to believe. But, moreover, as I have tried to show in this chapter, Abraham, as he is presented in *Fear and Trembling*, *knows* that Isaac will live. And he knows without his knowing cancelling or relieving his anxiety. In fact his knowing contributes to his anxiety. Not, of course, because it in some way sets up a reverberation of doubt. If that were so, Abraham would cease to have faith and his doubt would also rule out his knowing. Abraham's knowing intensifies his anxiety because it contributes to and deepens one of the sources of his anxiety that we have identified, namely, the second, his not being understandable to others. Abraham, as we have seen, can say *how* he knows Isaac will live: he has God's promise. Abraham has God's promise that through Isaac he will be the father of nations, and so Isaac must live, though he, Abraham, should bring down the knife. Yes, Abraham can say this, and it is indeed how he knows that Isaac will live. However, what he can say does not explain to others how he knows. To others it seems madness, for it is against common sense, it is absurd. Abraham, then, cannot communicate to those around him. While he can say words, he cannot explain how he knows, or why he is acting as he is. In this sense he must be silent.[6] And this necessary silence – this inability to make his knowing understandable to others, when he does indeed know, or to make understandable to others his actions predicated on that knowledge – further isolates him from the understanding of others and so intensifies his anxiety.

For Johannes de Silentio, it is easy to underestimate the extent of the isolation of silence that immures knights of faith. One knight of faith cannot help another, says Johannes.[7] This means that one knight cannot explain himself or herself even to another knight of faith. This is so, for Johannes, apparently because each faith relationship is an *individual* relationship. We may or may not go along with Johannes here – for, after all, it might seem that there could be some transfer from one individual faith relationship to another, and so some room for one knight's understanding of another. But, for Johannes, Abraham must be silent before even his wife Sarah.[8] Sarah, we may suppose, is also a knight of faith. Certainly, Johannes allows that she is. Nevertheless, Johannes insists, Abraham cannot explain even to Sarah what he would do, or what he has done, in following God's command. Even if we do not go along with Johannes here, and allow Abraham to communicate with Sarah, it would remain that Abraham will appear mad to the many others whom he meets in the world and will be opaque to their understanding.

Abraham is in anxiety as he follows God's command and takes his son to Moriah, but, we should appreciate, Abraham has anxiety as a part of his God-relationship even before his trial of faith. In his individual faith relationship to God he may be called upon *at any time* to do what is beyond the ethical and the understanding of others – what he must do by virtue of the absurd. Anxiety is a part of faith, on the *Fear and Trembling* model, not a mere concomitant of Abraham's instance of that faith during a particular critical episode in his life, although Abraham's anxiety in his trial of faith has the form and colouration it does because of the specific trial he undergoes. A constant source of anxiety for knights of faith is their unavoidable silence, their inability to make themselves understandable. Abraham, before he has God's command to take his son to the land of Moriah, may seem to others a dutiful father who loves his son with the same love they have for their sons; however, even then, Abraham must do everything he does by virtue of the absurd. For, even then, he, unlike his fellows, is outside the ethical. Abraham may act in accord with the ethical for years, and so be indistinguishable from others in his practice, but even then he is not following the ethical as they are. At any moment, in his individual relationship to God, he may be called upon to follow God's individual command to him and to act contrary to the ethical. Anxiety is left out of the story of Abraham, says Johannes de Silentio. Anxiety is left out of the story of Abraham's faith as it is manifested in his trial of faith, but also it is left out of the story of his faith in the quietude before his trial.

For Johannes, others can be like Abraham, and what makes another like Abraham is having faith. It is not having Abraham's individual relationship to God, but having Abraham's faith. That is, what makes one like Abraham is entering one's own individual faith relationship to God and having faith with the elements of Abraham's faith: no doubt, absolute trust, anxiety and joy. It is not murder that makes one like Abraham.[9] The direct object of Abraham's faith is that Isaac will live, not that I, Abraham, must kill Isaac. In fact, Abraham must believe and not doubt that he will *not* kill Isaac. Abraham, then, is very different from those who have come to believe that they have a duty or calling to kill others. Charles Manson, for instance, is not a candidate for one with Abraham's faith.[10] Others, however, may be.

Being like Abraham is having faith as Abraham did – sharing Abraham's faith of joyful knowledge, acted upon in anxiety and passionate trust. We should be clear that in order for one to have the faith that Abraham had it is not necessary that one be commanded by God to sacrifice one's son, or that one have a special promise from God that one will be a father of nations or, for that matter, any other special promise, such as the promise that one will prosper in one's calling or be successful in one's endeavours. Abraham had faith before he had God's promise that he would have a son Isaac and that through Isaac he would be the father of nations. His trial of faith takes the form it does, and comes to centre on his belief that God will not demand Isaac, because of the promise God has given Abraham. But Abraham was a knight of faith well before his ninety-ninth year, the year that God appeared to Abraham and promised that a son would be born to him and Sarah. Previous to God's promise, for many years, Abraham had walked before the Lord in faith (Gen. 12).

While the character of Abraham's faith is dramatically exhibited in his trial of faith, what makes Abraham the paradigmatic knight of faith is his faith, not his trial of faith. Nor is it that he received a special promise from God. It is being in a faith relationship to God, and what defines that faith is, importantly, a passionate trust and a joyful knowledge. In Abraham's case what he knows and rejoices in, in the trial of faith that God has given him, is – once again – precisely that Isaac will live. But this proposition is not the direct object of faith for other knights of faith, who are not Abraham. Yet any who have that faith that Abraham had are *ipso facto* knights of faith.

We have seen that Abraham, the paradigmatic knight of faith in *Fear and Trembling*, is joyful because he *knows* that all will be well, Isaac will live. Why God is testing him he may not know, but that Isaac will live he does know – and so he is joyful. That is, *within the story*, as retold by Johannes, Abraham has faith and knows that Isaac will live. Abraham knows that Isaac will live: this comment is an internal comment on the story and holds whether the story of Abraham is true or not. It holds if it is only a parable meant to express the demands of faith, which it would do if there had been no real Abraham, as the parable of the good Samaritan carries its moral and religious point whether or not there was an actual Samaritan being referred to by Jesus (Lk. 10:29–37).

To be sure, if we wish, we can raise the external question: Is the story true? And we can also raise the question: Can *anyone* in fact have the faith that Abraham had in Johannes' retelling, a faith which, if it is to be as it is presented in *Fear and Trembling*, must be characterized by a joyful *knowledge*? We shall take up this second question in Chapter 4. In the next chapter we shall try to bring out the dialectical contrast in *Fear and Trembling* between Abraham, the knight of faith, and the ethical hero, and also the contrast between the knight of faith and the knight of infinite resignation, and between the knight of faith and the demonic individual.

3

The Ethical, Infinite Resignation, and the Demonic

In *Fear and Trembling*, in that dimension of his 'Dialectical Lyric' that makes it dialectical, Johannes de Silentio juxtaposes the faith of the knight of faith, the faith of Abraham, to other states that are misleadingly similar to it. In doing so he brings into graphic relief the nature of faith against the background of what it is not. The three primary states with which he dialectically contrasts faith – the biblical faith of the *Fear and Trembling* model – are the ethical, infinite resignation, and the demonic. Each in its way is like faith, for faith shares something with each. Yet, though some would identify each of these three states with faith, none is faith. In this chapter I want to bring out the contrast between faith and each of these three states, as that contrast emerges in *Fear and Trembling*, and I want to do so with faith's joyfulness in mind. I shall take the three in order.

First, then, faith may be dialectically opposed to the ethical. The knight of faith may for much of his or her life never transgress the ethical, but at any time, as in Abraham's trial, the way of the knight may veer off from the way of the ethical. Moreover, even while the knight of faith does not transgress the ethical, the knight does not follow the ethical as the guide of his or her life. And, while there is a definite place for heroism in the ethical, the knight of faith is to be distinguished from the ethical hero.

What, for Johannes de Silentio, is the ethical? 'The ethical as such is the universal', says Johannes, 'and as the universal it applies to everyone.'[1] The ethical embodies duties that are binding on all. This is one important feature of the ethical. It has a second important feature: 'as the universal it is in turn the disclosed'.[2] Those who follow the ethical act in accord with a universal duty that is open to our common understanding. It is evident to us, and those of our

actions that are in accord with the ethical can be disclosed and ex-
plained to all, or nearly all. Those who consistently follow the
ethical, and thereby respect their ethical duty, are morally upright,
but they are not so far ethical heroes. Ethical heroes are those who
are faced with a moral conflict between a duty to one they love and
a higher moral duty that requires them to sacrifice what their heart
desires. They face a moral dilemma, and they rise to the higher
duty that, ethically, they must choose, though at the cost of their
own suffering and the loss of the one they love. They are essentially
tragic figures, and Johannes calls them 'tragic heroes'. He uses three
examples to illustrate the category, one biblical, one mythico-
literary, and one historical.[3] Johannes' biblical example is Jephthah
(Judges ll: 30–40); however, his mythico-literary and historical examples more than adequately illustrate his category. They are
Agamemnon and Lucius Junius Brutus.

King Agamemnon is the commander of the Greek forces that
have been assembled to besiege Troy. But the Greek ships are given
no favourable wind. It turns out that Artemis is angry with
Agamemnon and has becalmed the fleet. In the myth, as it is retold
by Euripides in *Iphigenia in Aulis* (which Johannes quotes),
Agamemnon sacrifices his daughter Iphigenia in order to appease
the goddess. Artemis accepts the sacrifice and allows the Greek
expeditionary force to sail.

The historical example of Lucius Junius Brutus is similar in the
relevant respects. Brutus, who is credited with being the founder of
the Roman republic, led the Romans in expelling the Tarquins
around the beginning of the sixth century BCE. The Tarquins,
however, oppose the new republic, and Brutus' sons help in the
plot for a Tarquinian restoration. His sons are apprehended, and
Brutus, as he must, executes them as rebels against the state.

In each case a father is called upon to sacrifice what he loves for
the sake of his higher ethical duty to protect and serve the state.
Though they are tempted not to do what their ethical duty requires,
they nevertheless rise to the occasion and with a heavy heart do
what they must. Tragic heroes never leave the ethical; they act in
accord with a higher ethical duty that is itself within the universal.
This means that their actions are understandable to us. Their
actions and sacrifice, Johannes says, elicit our sympathy and admiration. We understand the terrible moral choice they face and their
ethical courage in doing what their higher ethical duty requires. We
understand and sympathize with the agony of all tragic heroes, and

we at once have compassion and respect for these ethical heroes who rise to their higher duty with an ethical courage that many of us would fail to muster.

Abraham is different. He confronts a conflict of duties, but not between a lower and a higher ethical duty, both of which are within the universal. His conflict is between his ethical duty to his son and, if he is as he sees himself, a higher absolute duty to God. The first is within the universal, but the second is not.

Abraham, if he is to follow his absolute duty to God, must depart from the ethical: he must do what in its ethical expression is that he means to murder Isaac. So it is that there arises the question of 'a teleological suspension of the ethical', as it is put in *Fear and Trembling*.[4] If Abraham is as he sees himself, and as he is presented in Johannes' retelling of the story, there must be a teleological suspension of the entire ethical, a suspension of the ethical for the *telos* of his higher, absolute duty to God. If Agamemnon and Brutus are tempted, they are tempted by their heart's desire not to do what their ethical duty requires. If Abraham is tempted, he is tempted by the ethical itself.[5] His temptation is not to do as God commands but to do what ethics requires instead.

At the root of Johannes' contrast between the tragic hero and the knight of faith is the further idea that the ethical is distinguishable from higher and absolute obligations to God. This idea has seemed profoundly wrong to many. Among those who see it as ethically and religiously perverse is Martin Buber. Buber discusses the Kierkegaardian idea of a teleological suspension of the ethical in *Eclipse of God*. One thing that disturbs Buber is that Kierkegaard in *Fear and Trembling* does not consider the question 'Who is it whose voice one hears?'[6] This, as we have seen, is Sartre's question. As we have further seen, Kierkegaard, or rather Johannes, does not raise this question because Johannes is retelling the story of Abraham's trial in the light of a background story that assumes Abraham knows it is God who commands him to take Isaac to the land of Moriah. Finally, though, Buber agrees that Abraham can be confident that it is God's voice, for Abraham, he says, 'could not confuse with another the voice which once bade him leave his homeland and which he at that time recognized as the voice of God without the speaker saying to him who he was'.[7] Buber's greater concern lies elsewhere. His main concern is with the very concept of a teleological suspension of the ethical and what it would mean for the ethical; his concern is that if there is an absolute duty to

God, higher than the ethical, arising from an individual relationship to God, then ethics is 'relativised' and the universal ceases to
be 'universally valid'.[8]

Buber's concern is not without a basis. Before I speak to it, or let
Johannes de Silentio speak to it, let us note that Buber is not alone.
Milton Steinberg has said this:

> From the Jewish viewpoint – and this is one of its highest digni-
> ties – the ethical is never suspended, not under any circum-
> stances and not for anyone, not even for God. *Especially not for
> God*. Are not supreme Reality and supreme Goodness one and
> coessential to the Divine nature?[9]

Nor is this concern with the teleological suspension of the ethical
limited to Jewish thought. In the combined Judeo-Christian tradition
there have been several readings of the Abraham narrative. Louis
Jacobs finds three Jewish 'attitudes' toward the *Akedah*, 'the binding'
(of Isaac on the altar).[10] The first attitude that Jacobs identifies
stresses the story's happy ending. God tests Abraham, but there was
never a divine intention to let Abraham slay Isaac. And at the end
God commands Abraham *not* to kill Isaac. This is the interpretation
that Buber favours, I think.[11] A second attitude, 'very close to
Kierkegaard's attitude', stresses the command that God gave to
Abraham, which he must follow in fear and trembling. This interpretation allows that for Abraham God's command, and not the
ethical norm, is 'ultimate' and so allows a teleological suspension of
the ethical. A third Jewish attitude, identified by Jacobs, seeks to
combine the elements of the other two: God could never 'be false to
his own nature and command a murder, and yet *if* he could, then
Abraham would indeed be obliged to cross the fearful abyss'.

Jacobs' conclusion is that there are several equally authentic
Jewish views on the *Akedah*, some of which allow and some of
which reject the idea of a teleological suspension of the ethical.[12] A
similar point could be made about Christian thinking. It remains,
then, that there is, alongside Johannes' presentation of Abraham, a
strong religious intuition that there can be no teleological suspension of the ethical, that God cannot by His nature do or command
what is evil, what is contrary to the ethical goodness that He
himself embodies.

There is in *Fear and Trembling* an implicit resolution of this
concern about the relationship between the ethical and a higher ab-

solute duty to God, an implicit resolution of the ethical and religious concern about a teleological suspension of the ethical. At one point, in fact, in a critical passage, it draws near to becoming explicit.[13] In this passage Johannes says that the 'paradox of faith' is that the 'single individual is higher than the universal'. That is, he is saying, the absolute duty to God that arises from an individual's absolute relation to the absolute is higher than the duties of the ethical, which is the universal. Thus, we may conclude, the ethical as the universal is suspended in its application to the knight of faith Abraham, who stands in an individual and absolute relation to God. And so, Johannes goes on to say, the ethical 'is reduced to the relative', just as Buber says. But, says Johannes, 'from this it does not follow that the ethical should be invalidated; rather the ethical receives a completely different expression, a paradoxical expression'.

While Johannes does not explicitly say so, there are two senses of 'ethical' at work here. On the one hand there is the ethical as the universal with its two requirements: the obligations it contains bind all *and* they are disclosed to all, evident to all, or nearly all, in their specific requirements. Second, there is the ethical that is not invalidated by being given a paradoxical expression; the ethical in this second sense includes obligations – ethical obligations – that are paradoxical, which by definition are not disclosed, are not open to common understanding. Call the first the ethical$_1$ and the second the ethical$_2$.

The ethical$_1$, then, consists of only some obligations that individuals might have: those that are *both* binding on all *and* clear to all, while the ethical$_2$ consists of all obligations whether clear to all or not, whether paradoxical or not, and whether they do or do not arise from an individual relation to God.

The ethical$_1$ is 'universal' in the *Fear and Trembling* sense, with its two necessary conditions. The ethical$_2$ is universal in the sense that its obligations bind all who have them, but within the ethical$_2$ some individuals are bound by certain individual duties that may be far from evident to many. Notice that what distinguishes the ethical$_1$ from the ethical$_2$ is not that only in the ethical$_2$ are there duties that bind some and not others. There are ethical$_1$ duties of this sort as well. One such is the particular duty a person incurs by making a promise, which typically binds that person but no other. Another example – one significant for *Fear and Trembling* – is the duty a father has to love his son, which of course binds only those who are fathers. What separates the ethical$_1$ from the ethical$_2$ is that the former is wholly open and disclosed, while the latter is not, in that it includes obligations that are opaque to moral common sense.

Does Abraham do what is ethical? Following Johannes' implicit distinction, we should divide the question. No, we may reply, for he departs from the ethical$_1$. But yes, he does what is ethical in that he follows an obligation within the ethical$_2$. Abraham is in the ethical$_2$, but he is outside the ethical$_1$ by virtue of being not-disclosed: of necessity, if Abraham acts by virtue of the absurd he cannot be disclosed. The ethical for Johannes, as the 'universal' with its requirement of openness, is decidedly non-absurd. Abraham in the story follows his higher duty to God. Thus within the story he is beyond the ethical but not failing to follow his duty. Johannes is right: 'The story of Abraham contains ... a teleological suspension of the ethical.'[14] That is, it contains a teleological suspension of the universal, the ethical$_1$, but not a suspension of the ethical$_2$. In fact the *telos* for which the ethical$_1$ is suspended, or over-ruled, is Abraham's ethical$_2$ duty to God to do as He commands. Buber is right that the ethical is relativized, in the sense that it can be suspended, but it is the ethical$_1$ that is thus relativized. Johannes is also right that the ethical, the ethical$_2$, is not invalidated, for it is never suspended.

Abraham is following his duty to God. Is he doing so at the expense of his duty to love his son? Has his duty to God overruled his duty to love his son? No, it has not. Abraham can 'rest assured', says Johannes, that God does not demand of him that he actually hate Isaac. His absolute duty to God 'can never lead the knight of faith to stop loving'. Abraham 'must love Isaac with his whole soul'.[15] Ethically, ethically$_1$, Abraham meant to murder Isaac, for that is the only understanding open to common sense. But God did not command Abraham to murder Isaac. He could not, given His promise. And Abraham knows this, for he knows that Isaac will live. Abraham in his trial trusts God that all will be well for Isaac. And so Abraham acts in accord with his duty to God *and* in accord with his duty to love his son, even though that duty takes a para-doxical, ethical$_2$ expression. Abraham loves his son as much as, more than, Brutus loves his sons. But Brutus has our sympathy and admiration, for he, as a tragic hero, is within the universal and open to our understanding, while Abraham must proceed in anxiety without the understanding of his fellows.[16]

The ethical hero is sure and confident. Ethical heroes know that they are acting in accord with a superior ethical duty. Given what they are called upon to do by their superior ethical duty, they may, to be sure, proceed with trepidation. However, they are confident of their ethical duty. Abraham, the knight of faith, similarly has no doubt what his absolute duty to God is. It is not a difference between the tragic hero and the knight of faith that the tragic hero knows and the knight does not know. The difference between them, on this point of comparison, is that the confidence of the former is reinforced by everyone's sympathetic understanding, while Abraham is not understood. The tragic hero is tempted not to do what is ethical, but Abraham's temptation is to return to the ethical, the ethical$_1$, and its reassuring embrace of the sympathetic understanding of others. As long as he is the knight of faith, though, he is beyond this reassuring understanding. For the same reason he is even further from the approval of others. The tragic hero is a 'hero' in the straightforward sense of the word, but, as Johannes says, Abraham 'was no hero'.[17] (Johannes says at one point: 'I *think* myself *into* the hero; I cannot think myself into Abraham.')[18]

In other ways too the tragic hero is like and unlike the knight of faith. They are alike in that each is, at some level, following his or her higher duty, and in that each is prepared to make a sacrifice for the sake of what is higher. The difference, of course, is that the ethical hero remains within the ethical$_1$. It is essential for an Agamemnon or a Brutus that there be an ethical, an ethical$_1$, duty that calls for the sacrifice he makes. If there were not, he would be neither ethical nor a hero, but merely unethical, merely ethically lost. In this connection recall the third picture of Abraham in the Exordium.

In the third picture, we will recall, Abraham sees his willingness to sacrifice Isaac as a sin. The Abraham of the third picture sees things ethically, and what he was willing to do goes counter to ethics, ethics$_1$, for there is no higher ethical$_1$ duty that would justify what he did or meant to do. This Abraham cannot believe God's command is good, for it goes counter to the ethical. This Abraham would sacrifice himself in place of Isaac, which is ethically$_1$ allowable, but he cannot believe that he was doing as he ought in following God's command. Since there is no higher ethical$_1$ duty which he could be following he sees himself as ethically lost.

Tragic heroes, though, do have an identifiable higher ethical$_1$ duty and understand that they do. They are confident of their duty. At the same time they are *tragic* heroes. Here, given our concern, is the crucial contrast between the tragic hero and the knight of faith.

Brutus and Agamemnon suffer tragedy: they do what they ought at the cost of irretrievable personal loss. For them not all is well. They do their duty, but in the process they lose what their heart loves. They lose their children. Part of their heroism is that they give up their joy. Here they stand in irreconcilable contrast to the knight of faith, who has the joy of faith. Abraham is not a tragic figure; he is joyful – for he will not lose Isaac. Though it is by virtue of the absurd that he is joyful, his joyfulness pervades all that he does. For he knows that all will be well.

The second state with which faith contrasts is that of infinite resignation. 'Infinite resignation' is a category that Johannes de Silentio gives us, although this does not mean that it is made out of whole cloth. It is a recognizable religious category. What Johannes has in mind as infinite resignation embodies or at least resonates with the religious sensibility expressed in, 'not my will, but thy will be done'.

In infinite resignation one gives up what one wants most. This may be some special achievement or recognition that one greatly desires. It may be the recovery of one's child from a severe illness. It may be all of what one treasures in life. Infinite resignation, we should appreciate, is not the sour-grapes reaction, which in Aesop's fable the fox exhibits toward the unattainable grapes. It is not that attitude we assume when, realizing that something will not come to us, we tell ourselves that we did not really want it anyway. In the state of infinite resignation we reconcile ourselves to renouncing what we continue to want most in this world. Those who have attained infinite resignation renounce what they desire most, and while still desiring it attain a kind of peace and rest in renunciation.[19]

It *Fear and Trembling* there is an intimate relationship between infinite resignation and faith. For Johannes there are two movements of faith.[20] There is, as we might put it, a double movement of faith. The first movement is that of infinite resignation in which the knight of faith 'drains the deep sadness of life in infinite resignation'. In making the first movement the knight has not, so far, attained faith. It is the second movement that brings the knight to faith. In making it the knight 'grasp[s] everything again by virtue of the absurd'.[21] Each of the two movements has a religious significance for Johannes: each is a 'movement of infinity'.[22] In making the first movement alone, the movement of resignation, one 'cross[es] over into infinity'.[23] Then, in making the second movement, which is made only by virtue of the absurd, the knight makes the final leap to faith.[24]

In this way, for Johannes, the knight of faith passes through infinite resignation and then, by virtue of the absurd, makes another movement of infinity to faith. Moreover, for Johannes, the knight of faith makes this double movement of faith continually.[25] However, it is possible to stop at the stage of infinite resignation. It is possible to get no further. Attaining infinite resignation is no little thing, and many do not reach this stage, which is 'the last stage before faith'.[26] But in reaching this stage one may have 'use[d] all [one's] strength in resigning' and not be able to go further.[27] Those who attain infinite resignation, but get no further, are knights of infinite resignation. They are not commonplace and are a source of inspiration for others. If Abraham had attained only infinite resignation and had given up what he desired most, if he had said to God, 'I will give up my wish [not to lose Isaac]', then, still, 'he would have saved many', Johannes says.[28] He would have attained a kind of greatness, though he would not have attained faith. The hallmark of infinite resignation is that what is treasured most in life is given up.

Let us consider another example of infinite resignation provided by Johannes.[29] We are invited to imagine 'a young lad [who] falls in love with a princess, and this love is the entire substance of his life, and yet the relation is such that it cannot possibly be realized... .' If he can reconcile himself to giving up the princess he will have infinitely resigned himself to not having what has become the substance, the focus, of his life. In so doing he will not cease to love the princess, but his love for her will 'assume a religious character' and he will become 'reconciled with existence'. Though he will lose the princess, through his renunciation he will attain 'peace and rest'.

It is to be noted that in the case of the young man who loves the princess, as in the case of Abraham, there is a focus of life and existence. The whole of life has become 'concentrated' in one 'interest'. Any 'interest', says Johannes, 'can, if it proves unrealizable, prompt the movement of resignation'.[30] In addition to attaining the object of one's love, being admitted to law school, or seeing the recovery of one's child from illness, or any other specific desirable thing could become such a focus. But 'everything' can also be such a focus, for Johannes. In *Fear and Trembling* Johannes gives us a portrait of a contemporary knight of faith, a nineteenth-century urban dweller. As a knight of faith he too is 'continually making the movement[s] of infinity'. In fact it is in regard to this contemporary knight of faith that Johannes makes the point that knights of faith make the double movement of faith continually. However, it is not a part of Johannes' portrait of the contemporary knight of faith that the entire substance of his life resides in one discrete thing, such as attaining the love of a princess. What he gives up, or is prepared to give up, in his movement of resignation is 'everything'; it is the 'everything' of his life that is 'the most precious thing in the world'.[31] Similarly, Johannes, who presents himself as a knight of infinite resignation, renounces 'everything'.[32] It is, in short, as Johannes says, 'the whole temporal realm' that infinite resignation renounces,[33] whether as 'everything' or as some significant thing into which all of life has come to be concentrated.[34]

To attain infinite resignation one must make the required 'movement of infinity'. The one who is capable of making this movement, and does make it, but goes no further, becomes a knight of infinite resignation. He or she gains through resignation an 'eternal consciousness', which, for Johannes in his own infinite resignation, is his 'love for God'.[35] When this movement is made properly there is 'peace and rest', that spiritual peace that comes when all is given up to God. Moreover, this movement is made by one's own strength.[36] 'It takes a purely human courage to renounce the whole temporal realm', says Johannes.[37] It is, he allows, 'a purely philosophical movement'.[38] Though it is not an easy thing, it is a movement that any who can marshall their will can make. Knights of infinite resignation are sufficient to themselves.[39]

In their sublime resignation knights of infinite resignation are above the ills and disappointments of this world. They have given up already all that might tempt them. If the armour of their renunciation is unflawed, the temptations of what is desirable in the world can find no entry. It is not that they have ceased to desire what they have given up. Rather they have sacrificed what they desire most.

And so knights of infinite resignation have peace and repose, but if unexpectedly they should be given back what they have renounced, there is an awkwardness in their getting what they have given up. Johannes, when he tries to put himself in Abraham's place can imagine resigning himself to the loss of Isaac, but, he says, 'I would have spoiled the whole story, for if I had gotten Isaac

again, I would have been in an awkward position.'[40] For knights of
infinite resignation their peace derives precisely from their heroic
resignation, from their hard-won but completely accepted renunciation; and that peace, as Johannes sees, cannot tolerate a reversal of
fortune. It is important for the peace of resignation that it not be
troubled with what has been given up. If the father of the prodigal
son had been a knight of infinite resignation, he could not have received back his son with happy exuberance (Lk. 15:11–24). Again,
the peace and rest attained by knights of infinite resignation come
with their enduring the pain of not having what they have renounced; with their peace there is comfort, but it is 'comfort in
pain'.[41]

Johannes, while he cannot attain or even understand the faith of
Abraham, can, as we have seen, imagine being – and even presents
himself as being – a knight of infinite resignation. At the same time
he confesses to being a tragic hero; 'higher I cannot come', he says
in regard to his capacity as a tragic hero.[42] The two states are compatible, though neither necessitates the other. And neither is faith.
Furthermore, because infinite resignation is not faith, it is despair
(since in *Fear and Trembling*, as in other works in Kierkegaard's
pseudonymous corpus, what is not faith is despair). Yet the knight
of faith makes the movement of resignation continually, for he or
she makes both movements of infinity continually. This may
suggest that knights of faith are constantly falling into and emerging from despair. Clearly this is at odds with the portrait of faith in
Fear and Trembling. A small emendation is in order. We should understand the knight of faith's movement of infinite resignation,
which is in itself a part of his or her faith, as the knight of faith's
being prepared to give up all, as opposed to the knight's renouncing
all. Otherwise Abraham and every knight of faith must pass
through a state of non-faith, which is despair, on the way to faith,
and must do so continually. Abraham, then, continually makes the
first movement of infinity in that he is constantly prepared to give
up Isaac; but he never does give up Isaac, for he knows, by virtue of
the absurd, that Isaac will live.

Though not faith, infinite resignation is like faith in that it is a
movement of eternity. In making the first movement of faith, the
movement of infinite resignation, one gains an eternal consciousness, and one does so though one goes no further. The eternal
consciousness that Johannes attains through resignation, he says, is
his love for God. In his infinite resignation he transcends the

normal concerns of this world, and this is, or can be, a form of devotion to God. Robert Adams says that 'in *Fear and Trembling* the
movement of resignation, the sacrifice of the finite object of concentrated passion, is seen as constituting devotion to God'.[43] Johannes,
as a knight of infinite resignation, renounces 'everything'. What
greater devotion to God, and love for God, we might ask, than that
devotion that gives up all for God? We might even connect what
Johannes says about his love for God with the New Testament
passage 'Greater love has no man than this, that a man lay down
his life for his friends' (Jn 15:13).

However, infinite resignation is not faith. It is a kind of devotion
to God, or is when the knight of infinite resignation sacrifices to
God what he or she desires most, although it would seem that not
all instances of infinite resignation need be instances of such devotion to God, for one could renounce what one desires most, upon
realizing its unattainability, without sacrificing the object of desire
to God and, indeed, with no thought of God. In any case, whether
or not it is devotion to God, infinite resignation is not faith. For one
thing it does not embody in itself trust, as faith does. But the most
noteworthy difference, given the central concern of our enquiry, is
that infinite resignation has no place for joy. Johannes is very clear
on this point, as when he contrasts 'find[ing] rest in the pain of
resignation' with 'find[ing] joy by virtue of the absurd'.[44] Infinite
resignation brings peace and repose – but no joy.

Recall the second picture of Abraham in the Exordium. Abraham
in this picture takes Isaac to Mount Moriah, as God has commanded. There he silently arranges the firewood for the sacrifice
and binds Isaac. He does not hesitate. He is prepared to sacrifice his
son, in accord with God's command, though he must lose Isaac
thereby. This Abraham, who cannot believe that Isaac will not be
taken from him, has accommodated himself to the loss of Isaac.
When he returns home with Isaac, after sacrificing the ram, his
'eyes were darkened and he saw joy no more'. This Abraham we
can now recognize as a knight of infinite resignation. It may be, as
Johannes says, that if Abraham had been only a knight of infinite
resignation he would still have saved many. But he would not have
had faith, nor the joy of faith.

When Johannes imagines himself in the place of Abraham, he
imagines himself as a knight of infinite resignation, as we observed.
From the beginning he would have been resigned to losing Isaac.
'The moment I mounted the horse,' he says, 'I would have said to

myself: Now all is lost, God demands Isaac, I sacrifice him and along with him all my joy – yet God is love and continues to be that for me… .'[45] Johannes continues to love God, he says, but also he feels that 'all is lost'. The bitterness of Johannes' sentiment, like the bitterness of the Abraham in the second picture of the Exordium, is hard to deny. Infinite resignation, even when it is devotion to God, is or may be a bitter resignation. In any event, it is far from being joyful.

And so we come to the third state with which Johannes contrasts faith: the demonic. The demonic is a signal Kierkegaardian category that appears in more than one pseudonymous work. We find it, for instance, in *Either/Or*, in *The Concept of Anxiety*, and, notably, in *The Sickness unto Death*. It is always a state that in some way, or ways, is opposed to faith or to the religious. Of course this is not to say that the various pseudonymous authors understand the demonic and its opposition to the religious in the same way. The demonic in *Fear and Trembling* is for Johannes de Silentio a form of the aesthetic. It is, as it might be put, the apotheosis of the aesthetic. The aesthetic is another Kierkegaardian category found in various works. In *Fear and Trembling*, as in other works, the aesthetic is that mode of existence that seeks after what is immediately given in feeling and perception. It is not limited to appreciation of what is beautiful, although it may take that form, just as the aesthetic may express itself in an appreciation of, say, delicately seasoned food, or of anything given in immediate experience, including the objects of spectatorship. Reflective aesthetic individuals are not concerned with beautiful objects or fine food, or those things they might observe, for their own sake; rather, they are concerned with the play of their feelings and sensations elicited by beautiful objects, subtly seasoned food, and the objects of their spectatorship. This same reflective aesthetic concern can hold for much, or all, of one's life, including human relations. Aesthetic individuals, as such, savour their feelings and moods. In this way they are focused on themselves and their own experiences. In *Either/Or* 'The Seducer's Diary' is written by such an aesthetic individual.[46] One of Johannes de Silentio's demonic figures in *Fear and Trembling*, the merman, is also a seducer. However, while Johannes' treatment of the aesthetic is continuous with that in *Either/Or*, there are added elements in

Fear and Trembling. One is magnanimity. Magnanimity, especially as expressed in the magnanimous gesture done in secret, lends itself to the aesthetic temper: aesthetic individuals who do what is magnanimous in a hidden way can savour at once their generous act and the mystification of others caused by their secretiveness. Johannes, enlarging a case mentioned by Aristotle in the *Politics*, provides an example of such a magnanimous aesthetic individual. In Johannes' embellishment a bridegroom learns from the augurs that if he marries there will ensue a calamity that has its origin in his marriage. Having learned what is fated, the bridegroom has several options. He can keep silent and marry. If he does, he would be doing what is simply and straightforwardly unethical. The ethical reaction is to tell the bride, and not marry. The aesthetic reaction is not to marry, but not to tell the bride of the augur's message – the bridegroom would magnanimously save his bride-to-be, but also by withholding any explanation would surround his action with an air of mystery.[47] Though the bridegroom should choose the aesthetic course, he may not yet be demonic. In any case Johannes does not present the bridegroom as a demoniac. But Johannes' merman is presented as a demoniac. And the merman in his demonic reaction is similarly magnanimous. Johannes' merman is taken from the legend of Agnes and the merman.[48] The merman is a seducer and would seduce Agnes. As Johannes tells the story, however, Agnes by her innocence crushes the will of the merman. He renounces his intention and repents. At this point the merman can respond ethically and disclose himself, or he can remain hidden. If he inwardly repents, but also remains hidden, he surrenders to the demonic. Then he may try to save Agnes from her love for him by alienating her. Perhaps, Johannes says, he will 'incite all the dark passions in her' in order to belittle her and her love, and even to arouse her pride.[49] In this way, sparing himself no anguish, Johannes' demonic merman will save Agnes from her love for him.

The merman, unlike the tragic hero, and like the knight of faith, stands outside the universal. Demonic individuals are individuals and in this are like religious individuals: both are unlike those who abide by ethics$_1$. And both the demonic individual and the religious individual, the knight of faith, are in an 'absolute relation'. 'The demonic', says Johannes, 'has the same quality as the divine, namely that the single individual is able to enter into an absolute relation to it.'[50] But, of course, the demonic individual is absolutely related to the demonic, not the divine. In *Fear and Trembling* this does not mean that the demonic individual has an absolute faith relation to some satanic power or to evil. It means that the demonic individual has entered absolute relation to his or her own 'resolution', to his or her own will. This comes out most clearly in Johannes' treatment of Faust, another demonic figure, who 'holds to his resolution'.[51] Johannes' Faust is modelled on Goethe's, but once more Johannes takes some liberties. His Faust desires no honours; he 'tries as much as possible to walk in step with other men'; he does not see Margaret with the eyes of lust; and he has 'a sympathetic nature'.[52] He is sympathetic toward humanity, and he would do good for humankind. In this, Johannes' Faust is like the merman and some other demonic figures.[53] In fact, with the merman in mind, Johannes says, 'in a certain sense there is ever so much more good in a demoniac than in superficial people'.[54] To be sure, demoniacs may choose to do evil: Bluebeard and Shakespeare's Richard III are also demoniacs.[55] But their choosing evil is not what makes them demoniacs. Also Johannes' Faust is a doubter, though Johannes allows that this too is not essential.[56] For Johannes what makes demoniacs demonic is not their doubt, if they do doubt, nor is it their doing evil, which they may perhaps not do. It is their absolute relation to their resolution, their will, that is essential.

One other point of similarity between demonic figures and knights of faith should be mentioned, one that is of great importance for Johannes de Silentio. Demonic individuals, like knights of faith, are silent. Faust and the merman do not speak: they do not explain themselves. The silence of the demonic parallels the silence of faith. But it is significantly different. Unlike the inescapable silence of faith, the silence of the demonic is chosen. The merman chooses to inclose himself and to save Agnes with the deceptive devices of his cunning. However, he can explain himself if he chooses.[57] If the merman speaks and openly repents then he enters the universal, he becomes ethical and open to the understanding of others, including Agnes. This he can do, though he rejects the ethical in choosing the demonic state and its silence.[58] Abraham is different: he cannot speak. His silence is not aesthetic.[59] He does not choose to remain silent. He must be silent, for, as he acts by virtue of the absurd, no words that he might utter can explain his actions to any other.

Abraham in the first picture of the Exordium is demonic. In the first picture, we recall, when Isaac begs for his life, Abraham tries to deceive him, but he does so for Isaac's own good. 'I am not your father', he tells Isaac; 'I am an idolator.' He reasons it is better that Isaac should go out of this world believing his father a monster than that Isaac should lose his faith in God. This Abraham is magnanimous in his self-abnegation and anguish, even as the merman was, and his deceptive means are similar. And this Abraham serves not the will of God, which he no longer trusts, but his own resolution.

The demonic individual and the knight of faith are superficially alike, then, in their both having an absolute relation, in their both being outside the universal, and in their both being silent. The differences between them are that the demoniac is absolutely related to the demonic, while the knight of faith is absolutely related to the divine; the demoniac is outside the universal, or ethics$_1$, and may also be outside ethics$_2$, while the knight of faith is outside ethics$_1$ but within ethics$_2$; and the demoniac can speak, while the knight of faith cannot.

And what of the joyfulness of the demonic? Faust, even Johannes' Faust, Richard III, and the merman seem mired in their anguish and pain, as does Abraham in the first picture of the Exordium. Could other conceivable demonic figures be joyful? That is, could individuals who qualify as demonic, as Kierkegaard uses that term, be joyful? Could some who serve their will absolutely embody a sense of joyfulness, perhaps born of their accomplishment and work? In asking these questions, particularly the last, we again draw near to our core concern with the relationship between the joyful acceptance of faith in *Fear and Trembling* and the joyful acceptance of life embodied in Nietzsche's Zarathustra. For the present I shall leave these questions open.

4

Knights of Faith

Abraham is the paradigmatic knight of faith, but for Johannes de Silentio he is not therefore the first and last knight of faith. In Chapter 2 I suggested that Abraham's wife Sarah might also be a knight of faith. For Johannes, in fact, there may be many knights of faith. He says that he does not deny that every second person may be a knight of faith.[1] Johannes not only may, but must, allow this possibility, given the character of faith presented in *Fear and Trembling*. Faith, finally, is a matter of an individual faith relationship between the religious individual and God, an individual relationship which, along with the requirements it imposes, may be invisible to others. Many, then, for all Johannes or anyone can tell, may be knights of faith by virtue of such an individual faith relationship to God. Every second person may have an individual calling, not visible to others, that he or she as a religious individual follows. Though knights of faith, many knights might seem quite ordinary morally, for they would appear to be following the ethical$_1$. And, in fact, for much of their lives they might well act in accord with the ethical$_1$, although the absolute requirements of their individual faith relationships may at any time lead these religious individuals, like Abraham, to veer off from the ethical$_1$.

In this connection recall the story of the rich young man in the New Testament. He asks Jesus what he must do to have eternal life, and Jesus tells him he must keep the commandments: 'You shall not kill. You shall not commit adultery. You shall not steal. You shall not bear false witness. Honour your father and mother, and, You shall love your neighbour as yourself.' All these he has done, says the young man. 'What do I still lack?' he asks. And Jesus says to him, 'If you would be perfect, go, sell what you possess and give to the poor, and you will have treasure in heaven; and come, follow me' (Matt. 19:16–21). In saying these words Jesus calls the young man and invites him to enter an individual faith relationship to Him, one that has the requirement that the young man sell all that he possesses. In the biblical story the young man cannot bring

45

himself to do as Jesus asks, and so he goes away in sorrow. However, imagine that the young man does as Jesus tells him to do, and that he follows Jesus. In doing so he would enter an individual faith relationship to Him. He would become a knight of faith in an individual relationship to God, and in following the duties of that relationship – in selling all that he has – he would depart from the ethical$_1$. So, if the young man had done as Jesus asked, like Abraham, he would have been a knight of faith acting by virtue of the absurd beyond the ethical$_1$. While this much seems fairly evident, it must be confessed that my depiction of the rich young man is at odds with what Johannes says about him. Johannes says that though we would praise the young man if he sold all his possessions and even find him hard to understand, still he would be unlike Abraham. Unlike Abraham, Johannes suggests, the young man would not go beyond the ethical – the ethical$_1$ – in selling all his possessions and giving the money to the poor, for, says Johannes, 'to money I have no ethical [ethical$_1$] obligation'.[2] One can see Johannes' point, but I do not think that it is quite right. While there may be no ethical obligation to money *per se*, there are ethical obligations to provide for family and to use our money wisely, so that donated money goes to a good use and we do not make ourselves or our dependants indigent in the process. Many, I think, would recognize these ethical obligations, which is to say that they are ethical$_1$ obligations. Jesus in effect is giving the young man an absolute duty that teleologically suspends these ethical$_1$ obligations. Relevant here is what happens later at the Passover in Bethany at the house of Simon the leper, as the story is rendered in Matthew (Mt. 26:6–13), or at the house of Lazarus, as the story is rendered in John (Jn 12:1–5). There, in Bethany, a woman anoints Jesus with a costly ointment. Jesus' disciples are indignant, morally indignant, for they view this as a waste: the money spent on the ointment might have been put to better use. These 'disciples' (in the version in John, Judas Iscariot) are ethically dismayed in the light of the ethical$_1$ obligation, while Jesus regards the anointment as a beautiful act (Mt. 26:10). Allowing that these disciples reflect a commonsense understanding of what is morally right, that is, an ethical$_1$ understanding, and allowing that the woman who anoints Jesus (Mary in Jn 12:3) is acting as she ought in accord with her faith relationship to Jesus, she is not violating the ethical$_1$ but is beyond it. Similarly, allowing that the rich young man, from a commonsense ethical standpoint, can be accused of not putting his money to 'good use' if he sells all that he has and simply gives the money to the poor, he too would be beyond the ethical₁ in the manner of a knight of faith.

Arguably, then, the rich young man of the New Testament, if he had done what Jesus asked him to do, would have gone beyond the ethical – the ethical₁ – and would have been acting by virtue of the absurd as a knight of faith. Whether or not the rich young man qualifies as a knight of faith, however, others, many others, do or may. So Johannes allows in *Fear and Trembling*. In *Fear and Trembling*, as I observed in the last chapter, Johannes de Silentio provides us with a portrait of a contemporary knight of faith. Johannes has never, to his knowledge, seen a knight of faith, although, he says, he has been looking for many years.[3] While he may never have encountered a knight of faith, still, Johannes reflects, he can imagine one. And so it is that he imagines and brings forth a knight of faith, a contemporary living in his, or Kierkegaard's, own Copenhagen. What is Johannes' imagined knight of faith like? His portrait is not lacking in detail.[4] The knight he imagines appears to be very ordinary, hardly distinguishable from other citizens one might see walking along the street. He looks like a tax-collector. He walks along with a steady gait, like a postman. Perhaps he is a clerk, who attends to his work dutifully – or one might take him to be a merchant. As he walks along, he seems comfortable enough in his surroundings, like a man out for a pleasant stroll in the park on a Sunday afternoon: indeed, observes Johannes, 'he belongs entirely to the world; no bourgeois philistine could belong to it more'. He takes pleasure in all that he sees. He enjoys a walk in the woods, but also he enjoys watching the new omnibuses, recently introduced on the streets of Copenhagen, and the crowds of city-dwellers. As he walks home he anticipates the hot meal that his wife will have for him, for he has a good appetite. Perhaps she will have prepared something special. But it is all the same to him that she has not. He attends church, but there too he does not stand out and is indistinguishable from other parishioners.

In short, nothing in the outward demeanour of the contemporary knight of faith shows him to be a knight of faith. Yet, we are to understand, he has the faith of Abraham. Like Abraham, he acts and believes by virtue of the absurd, endures anxiety, believes for this world, has no doubt, trusts God that all will be well, *knows* that all will be well, and is joyful in his faith. Like Abraham, the contemporary knight of faith 'continually' makes the two movements of infinity, the double movement of faith: he continually 'drains the deep sadness of life in infinite resignation [and then grasps] everything again by virtue of the absurd'.[5] As with Abraham, the contemporary knight of faith has faith for *this* world: as Abraham does not believe that he will get a second Isaac in a future life, but that the Isaac he loves in this world will not be lost to him, so the contemporary knight of faith believes for this world. The 'everything' that he gives up, or rather, is prepared to give up, in infinite resignation, and then grasps again in the movement of faith, is the everything of this life – he 'belongs to this world', as Johannes says.[6]

And the contemporary knight of faith, like Abraham, has an individual faith relationship to God. This means that, while he may appear to be comfortably bourgeois, at any time his faith relationship may require him to do what is beyond the ethical₁, or universal, and will not be understandable to his fellows. Though he may seem to have the same relationship to the universal as others, in fact he does not. This at every point is a source of anxiety. As a knight of faith, he, like Abraham, suffers the anxiety that faith necessitates.

The contemporary knight of faith is a knight of faith by virtue of having the faith that Abraham exemplifies. But this is not to say that he is like Abraham in every respect. He need not be in order to have the faith of Abraham. Notably he is not called upon to sacrifice his son. Nor does he have a promise from God that through his son he will be the father of nations. What makes Abraham the father of faith is his faith, not his trial of faith. To be sure, in that trial the depth and character of Abraham's faith become most evident. Still, it is his faith, which is tried, not the trial of his faith, that makes Abraham a knight of faith; and it is Abraham's faith, not his trial, that the contemporary knight of faith must share.

Like Abraham, the contemporary knight of faith must have absolute trust in God, but his absolute trust is unlike Abraham's in that it does not rest upon God's special promise. The contemporary knight of faith has not been promised by God that he will have a son, nor has God appeared to him and promised him wealth or health or anything else. This means that the direct object of the faith of the contemporary knight of faith, what he knows and does not doubt, must be different from the direct object of Abraham's faith. Going beyond *Fear and Trembling*, we can identify it as the belief that all will be well. The direct object of Abraham's faith was that

Isaac will not be lost to him: it was, we may say, that all will be well with Isaac. The direct object of the faith of the contemporary knight of faith is the more general belief that all will be well – all will be well with 'everything', the everything he is prepared to give up and grasps again by virtue of the absurd. As Abraham's conviction that he will not lose Isaac connects to, expresses, and is required by his faith and trust in God, so the contemporary knight's conviction that all will be well connects to, expresses, and is required by his faith and trust in God.

Here, admittedly, we go beyond Kierkegaard's *Fear and Trembling*, but not beyond the religious tradition, or traditions, in which Kierkegaard, Johannes, and Abraham stand. In the Bible there is the story of the Shunammite woman and the prophet Elisha. The Shunammite woman recognizes Elisha as a man of God and is generous to him: she gives him food and a place to rest. Elisha in return prophesies that, though she is old, in a year's time she shall have a son. This happens, but while the child is still young, an illness descends upon him and he dies. Immediately she prepares to go to Elisha, telling her husband that it will be well. When she comes before Elisha, he asks, 'Is it well with you? Is it well with your husband? Is it well with the child?' And she answers, 'It is well' (2 Kings 4:8–26). With these words she affirms her faith and her trust.[7] Julian of Norwich in the fourteenth century echoes the words of the Shunammite woman. In her *Showings*, writing of what was revealed to her in her vision of Christ, Julian says of Jesus that 'He comforts readily and sweetly with his words, and says: But all will be well, and every kind of thing will be well.'[8] The direct object of faith for the contemporary knight of faith, then, we may allow, is just this belief that all will be well, which as a knight of faith he believes with no diminishment of doubt.

Whence this certainty? Its source cannot be in the kind of revelatory promise that was given to Abraham. Nor can its source very well be in the kind of consciousness-wrenching religious vision that Julian of Norwich had in her thirty-first year. On the other hand, I think that we may posit a sense of God's presence as the source of the certitude of the contemporary knight of faith. Like the Psalmist, and others in various religious traditions, the contemporary knight of faith may have experienced God's presence in his daily life and felt God's goodness in His creation.[9] In making this suggestion once again I go beyond Johannes' vignette of the contemporary knight of faith, but I add to it without contradicting it. For

Johannes, faith is not immediate: what is believed in faith is not given immediately, as what is sensible is immediately given to the senses. Yet, for Johannes, as he says, though 'faith is not the first immediacy, [it is] a later immediacy'.[10] Similarly, Johannes Climacus in the *Postscript* on the one hand insists that 'immediate religiousness rests in the pious superstition of seeing God directly in everything'[11] and on the other hand says that, though 'not even God relates himself directly to a derived spirit', nevertheless 'within the individual human being there is a possibility ... that in inwardness is awakened to a God-relationship, and then it is possible to see God everywhere'.[12] For both these pseudonymous authors, then, it is possible to 'see' God everywhere, to come into God's presence in all of His creation – but only after entering into the God-relationship of faith. I do not know that we have to agree with Kierkegaard that seeing God in His creation can come only *after* faith. (Why should we deny that one might come to have faith precisely because one has discovered God's presence?) However, this much is clear: Kierkegaard allows that the contemporary knight of faith has experienced God's presence. Accordingly, we may posit this experience as the basis of the knight's certitude that all will be well, even if, for Kierkegaard, that basis is only attainable with faith.

Perhaps the greatest or most notable difference between Abraham and the contemporary knight of faith is this: Abraham has a crucial trial of faith while the contemporary knight of faith, in Johannes' presentation, is not portrayed in a trial of his faith. As I pointed out, faith does not require a trial of faith. Still this difference is striking, and it raises the question: What would be a similar trial of faith for the contemporary knight of faith? Such a trial of faith can be imagined, I think, and consistently added to Johannes' picture of the knight, once that picture is filled out in the way I have suggested. Once we identify as the direct object of the contemporary knight's faith the belief that all will be well, parallel to Abraham's belief that Isaac will not be lost to him, we can go on to imagine a parallel trial of faith.

The contemporary knight of faith, Johannes says, continually makes the movements of infinity, grasping everything again by virtue of the absurd in the movement of faith. The knight, then, we may say, is constantly resigning himself to giving up everything and constantly grasping back everything in his conviction, held by virtue of the absurd, that all will be well. This he does continually. But as long as his life flows its normal easy course, there is no trial of his conviction and faith. Say, though, that disaster strikes. Say that he loses all. Imagine him to be like Job. He loses his livelihood, his family and finally his health. Say that this is his trial of faith. Yet, if he continues to have faith, he will trust in God and praise God and thank God. He will, for he knows that all is well. And how does he know? When he lifts up his eyes he sees God's goodness all about him. But this is absurd: like Abraham, if he knows, he knows by virtue of the absurd. Like Abraham he will be far beyond human calculation and understanding. To human calculation he will appear to be mad. For human calculation, it is time to curse God and die (Job 2:9).

Knights of faith can appear commonplace, as Abraham, rich and comfortable with his flocks of sheep, may have seemed before his own trial of faith, and as the contemporary knight of faith appears, walking down the boulevard with a confident gait. But this is before their trials. In their trials they exhibit the depth of their trust and they depart from the understanding of common sense. Common sense, the sense of things common to human calculation, urges Abraham to repent his unethical behaviour, for so it regards what Abraham would do. And common sense urges the contemporary knight of faith, in our expanded construction, to renounce God and embrace death (or at least to give up trusting God). Because knights of faith are continually prepared to trust absolutely they are, even before their trials, at odds with common sense and believe by virtue of the absurd – Abraham, before his trial, is prepared to believe that Isaac will not be lost to him though God should call upon him to sacrifice his son; and the contemporary knight of faith, before the trial we have imagined, is prepared to trust in God and His goodness though he should suffer the torments of Job. Note that this opposition between common sense and the demands of faith does not mean Abraham does not know that Isaac will live or that the contemporary knight of faith does not know that all will be well. Nor does it mean that they cannot say how they know: Abraham can say, 'I know for I have God's promise' and the contemporary knight of faith can say, 'I know for I see God's goodness in His presence all about me.' However, as we have seen, though such words can be uttered – and though they do indeed say how the knights know, if they know – such words do not explain; they do not serve to communicate, and the knights, in this way, are consigned to an inescapable silence. This is as much true of the contemporary knight of faith as it is of Abraham.

In the imagined trial of faith that we have given him we have made the contemporary knight of faith Job-like. How did Kierkegaard regard Job? Did he regard him as a knight of faith? Though Job is not mentioned in *Fear and Trembling*, Kierkegaard does mention him, and even dwells upon him, in an 'upbuilding discourse' that he published in 1843. Two months after publishing *Fear and Trembling* Kierkegaard published *Four Upbuilding Discourses* (1843). This volume of discourses, like the other collections of discourses he published, is signed by Kierkegaard. In it, then, Kierkegaard speaks without the intervening voice of a pseudonym. One of the four discourses in this volume, 'The Lord Gave, and the Lord Took Away: Blessed Be the Name of the Lord', is a meditation on Job – Job, who blesses the name of the Lord out of the midst of his suffering (Job 1:21). Though Kierkegaard does not say that Job is a knight of faith – that category belongs to the pseudonymous Johannes – he does speak of Job's 'incorruptible joy' and affirms that when Job says 'Blessed be the name of the Lord' he 'witnesses to joy'.[13] Joyfulness, for Johannes de Silentio, is the hallmark of faith, and, in ways I tried to bring out in Chapter 2, connects to the confidence, trust and certainty of faith in its *Fear and Trembling* construction. We may observe, then, that, though Kierkegaard does not say so, Job in Kierkegaard's discourse exhibits what Johannes de Silentio recognizes as a central feature of faith: a joyfulness even in the midst of tribulation.

On the day that Kierkegaard published *Fear and Trembling* he also published another pseudonymous work. That work is *Repetition*, and its author is Constantin Constantius. One section of the book consists of letters Constantin Constantius received from a young man he knows, who is referred to simply as 'The Young Man'. The Young Man in several letters reflects on Job, and, while we need not go further into *Repetition*, it is useful to note what he says about Job.

The Young Man in one letter compares himself to Job in his loss: he has lost his beloved and, he says, he has lost his 'honor and pride and along with it the vitality and meaning of life'.[14] How does the Young Man regard Job? He is struck by Job's wanting to defend himself before God (Job 13:3 and 15). As the Young Man sees Job, the latter is bringing his complaint to God and defending his despair.[15] The Young Man approaches Job with confidence, boldness, and trust, more than any other figure in the Old Testament, 'simply because he is so human in every way'.[16] In seeing Job as being in despair, which is the denial of faith, the Young Man cannot regard him as a living example of faith, and, accordingly, he trusts him just for being 'so human', as opposed to standing in awe before his faith. But this is not surprising, for the reaction of the Young Man to Job is essentially aesthetic. 'Every time I come to it [the Book of Job],' he says, 'it is born anew as something original or becomes new and original in my soul. Like an inebriate, I imbibe all the intoxication of passion little by little, until by this prolonged sipping I become almost unconscious in drunkenness.'[17]

While the Young Man appreciates that Job is not demonic (as he would be, the Young Man sees, if he loved God for the sake of his own nobility),[18] and while he appreciates that Job is undergoing an 'ordeal' (that is, a spiritual trial like Abraham's, although the Young Man does not make the connection),[19] he nevertheless cannot see Job as a 'hero of faith'. 'Job's significance', for him, 'is that the disputes at the boundaries of faith are fought out in him, that the colossal revolt of the wild and aggressive powers of passion is presented here.' And 'for this reason Job does not bring composure as does a hero of faith'.[20]

At the end of *Repetition*, in a concluding letter offered to the reader, Constantin Constantius says of the Young Man: 'If he had had a deeper religious background, he would not have become a poet. Then everything would have gained religious meaning.'[21] If the Young Man had had a deeper religious sense, then he might have escaped the aesthetic preoccupation of a poet and seen the religious significance of 'everything'. Constantin Constantius may have in mind *repetition* specifically: the Young Man thinks of it in the worldly terms of regaining what he has lost – his honour and pride – and not as a religious repetition, which relates to the eternal. However, Constantin Constantius' reflection extends as well to the Young Man's understanding of Job, we may allow. It is because the Young Man does not have a deep religious sense that he cannot understand Job to be an exemplar of faith and sees Job's suffering and his crying out to God as despair. Of course it would remain that Constantin Constantius' comment on the Young Man, and on his understanding of Job, allowing that it is that, is the comment of one pseudonymous author on another, as opposed to Kierkegaard's own direct comment. But his comment would fit with the reading of Kierkegaard's discourse on Job that I have suggested.

In Kierkegaard's journals and papers there is a further comment on Job that is relevant to our understanding of Job as a possible knight of faith. It is in a paragraph of material that Kierkegaard deleted from the final copy of *Concluding Unscientific Postscript*, the pseudonymous work by Johannes Climacus:

> That the discourse on Job is different from the others is clear enough.... The basis of the distinction the Magister [i.e. Magister Kierkegaard] himself has communicated to me [i.e. Johannes Climacus]. In the book *Repetition*, the use of Job was so caught up in passion that it could easily have a disturbing effect on one or another reader so accustomed to something more quietly up-building in a consideration of the devout man. Therefore he immediately decided to do his best to keep Job as a religious prototype.... [And] the upbuilding discourse also appeared a few weeks after *Repetition*.[22]

What is to be noted here is the designation of Job as 'a religious prototype'. Again this is the comment of a pseudonymous author, Johannes Climacus, and, moreover in a paragraph that did not appear in the *Postscript*. Still, it perhaps reflects Kierkegaard's intention to 'keep Job as a religious prototype' which is once more in accord with our reading of his discourse on Job.[23]

It seems to me, then, that we can fill out the portrait of the contemporary knight of faith by making him Job-like without departing from either the religious perspective that informs *Fear and Trembling* or from the parallel and complementary strain of Kierkegaard's non-pseudonymous religious reflections. In this way we obtain a full picture of a knight of faith other than Abraham. Are there other candidates who might be brought forward? We can, I think, glean at least two other examples from *Fear and Trembling*. One is the Virgin Mary.[24] She is like Abraham, says Johannes, in her greatness, which, as with Abraham, arises not from what happened to her, but from what she did. It arises not from her being the favoured one among women, but from how she proceeds. She is a virgin with child. Can she explain this to anyone? She can utter the words that an angel has announced to her that she will bear a child, conceived by the Holy Spirit, who will be the Son of God (Lk. 1:26–31). But these words, like all of Abraham's words, fail to explain. Mary, like Abraham, is immured in silence. It is for this reason that, as Johannes says, no one can understand her. And, like Abraham, she must therefore proceed in anxiety. This too Johannes brings out. Johannes does not explicitly call Mary a knight of faith. But all the elements are present – those Johannes brings out and those he leaves unspoken. Although Johannes does not make it explicit, Mary, like Abraham, believes and acts by virtue of the absurd. She trusts God absolutely. She is joyful in the knowledge that she has been chosen.

The other example of a knight of faith provided by Johannes de Silentio is Sarah in the Book of Tobit.[25] In the Apocrypha, in the Book of Tobit, there is the story of Tobit's son Tobias and Sarah. Tobias would marry Sarah. However, Sarah has been given to seven husbands and each has died in the bridal chamber, for she is cursed by a demon who loves her and kills each bridegroom on his wedding night. Tobias, though, is told by the angel Raphael how the demon can be exorcised by magic. Tobias marries Sarah and on their wedding night banishes the demon. The spell is broken. Sarah and Tobias pray to the Lord, asking for mercy and that they may grow old together as husband and wife. And so they do. Thus the Book of Tobit (6:9–8:8 and 14:12–13). Johannes keeps the story intact in its essence, although he makes Sarah 'a girl who has never been in love' in order to avoid the 'comic effect' of her 'seven futile attempts to get married', and he waves the angel Raphael offstage. Again, in Johannes' version, though she has never been married, Sarah is under a curse, and there is a demon who will kill her bridegroom on their wedding night. Tobias knows this, but he loves her. Courageously, he marries her. This is as much of the story as Johannes needs.

While Johannes is sure that a poet, if he were to use this story, would celebrate the heroic courage of Tobias, he, Johannes, is drawn to Sarah. 'Sarah is the heroic character', he reflects:

> For what love of God it takes to be willing to let oneself be healed when from the very beginning one in all innocence has been botched, from the very beginning has been a damaged specimen of a human being! What ethical maturity to take upon oneself the responsibility of permitting the beloved to do something so haz-

ardous! What humility before another person! What faith in God that she would not in the very next moment hate the man to whom she owed everything![26]

In his exclamation Johannes acknowledges Sarah's faith, but then, for Johannes, she must be a knight of faith. Also she is heroic and has 'ethical maturity'. Does this make her a tragic hero? No, for as a knight of faith she must be beyond the ethical, the universal. As we have seen, Johannes needs and uses – though he does not explicitly draw – a distinction between the ethical$_1$ and the ethical$_2$. Sarah has the ethical$_2$ maturity of an Abraham, beyond the common understanding of those around her, as opposed to the ethical$_1$ heroism of a tragic hero, which is open to universal approval and understanding, and which Tobias enjoys – for his courage, unlike Sarah's moral strength, is evident to the many and is generally applauded. In what sense is she heroic, then? She is a hero by virtue of her greatness, not a hero in the sense that she is open to the acclaim and admiration of many.[27]

If we go beyond *Fear and Trembling* we might find many other examples of knights of faith. Job would qualify, I have suggested. Moses and many of the prophets of the Old Testament might also be candidates. In these cases we have biblical descriptions of their individual relationships to God and the requirements of their individual relationships. Consequently, as long as our judgement about their knighthood is an internal judgement, we have much to help us. Might there be others, actual persons, who are contemporary knights of faith, contemporary with Kierkegaard in the nineteenth century or contemporary with us in the twentieth or twenty-first? This of course is a harder question, for it is not an internal question relating to a story. We might think of, for instance, Albert Schweitzer or Dietrich Bonhoeffer as religious individuals who might be knights of faith. But the very fact that they are religiously and ethically impressive to us may tell against them. Only if we can transcend ethics$_1$ and, looking into a human life, judge that another person is acting in accord with a higher, ethical$_2$ duty can we come to a judgement that that person is a knight of faith – something, we will recall (from Chapter 2), that Johannes de Silentio says even one knight of faith cannot tell about another knight of faith. But also, we should recall, Johannes says that, for all he knows, every second person may be a knight of faith.

Part II

5

Nietzsche as the Antichrist

Nietzsche sometimes signed his letters 'Dionysus'. In his first book, *The Birth of Tragedy*, published in 1872, he argued that alongside the Apollonian in Greek culture there was a more profound Dionysian strain. For Nietzsche, the Dionysian, in contrast to the Apollonian, is alive to instinct; and it carries within itself an insight into the darkness of life. Dionysian is the sense of tragedy and the emotional release of dithyrambic music. Nietzsche could easily accept these attributes as attributes of his own character – not that the only persona he assumed was that of Dionysus. As he would sometimes sign himself 'Dionysus', so he could and did also sign himself 'The Antichrist'. In 1888 he wrote, and in 1895 he published, *The Antichrist*. His choice of title is calculated, for Nietzsche wishes to be as provocative as he can.[1] In this book he argues against religion and against Christianity specifically. He speaks as an anti-Christian, but, more than that, he assumes the identity of the Antichrist, the dedicated and unrelenting enemy of Christianity. (*Der Antichrist* is the German expression for 'the Antichrist', but since the German for 'Christian', masculine, is *Christ*, *Der Antichrist* can mean both 'the anti-Christian' and 'the Antichrist'; without qualification, the German term would normally be taken to mean the apocalyptic Antichrist.) It is as 'The Antichrist' that Nietzsche signed his 'Decree Against Christianity', written in 1888 as an addendum to *The Antichrist*.[2]

Both Kierkegaard and Nietzsche criticize the religion of their respective eras. In writing *Fear and Trembling* and the *Postscript* Kierkegaard implicitly criticizes the religion of his contemporaries, for in these works he presents models of faith that are more demanding than the socially approved Christianity of his day. During the last phase of his writing Kierkegaard became more explicitly critical: in the last year of his life he launched into what has been called his 'attack upon "Christendom"'. In this phase, through satirical articles and broadsides, Kierkegaard speaks directly and harshly against the religion of his contemporary

Denmark – and the established Lutheran Church of Denmark. What it considers faith, Kierkegaard perceives, is a watered-down, habitual belief with no hard consequences for one's life, a comfortable belief which it is socially profitable to confess in public. Kierkegaard's criticism is not of Christianity; it is of 'Christendom'. It is not of faith; it is that what is called faith is not faith.

Nietzsche's criticism is different. To be sure, Nietzsche, like Kierkegaard, criticizes the form that Christianity has come to have. For Nietzsche, Christianity has been perverted by Paul and by the priests. But also, for Nietzsche, Christianity itself is a perversion. 'War to the death against depravity', he wrote, and, he continued, 'depravity is Christianity'.[3] Nietzsche's criticism is of the Christianity of his day, but also it is of Christianity itself. It is of what passes for faith and of faith itself.

If one had to express Nietzsche's criticism of Christianity in a word, it would be this: Christianity negates life. Such a summing up, however, does not do justice to either the diversity or the subtlety of Nietzsche's thinking. For Nietzsche, Christianity's opposition to life manifests itself variously. He sees it, for instance, in Christianity's 'hatred of the senses'. 'Christian', he says, 'is the hatred of the *senses*, of joy in the senses, of joy itself.'[4] Given our underlying concern in this book with the place given to joy and to joyful acceptance by Kierkegaard and by Nietzsche, this aspect of Nietzsche's criticism of Christianity is worthy of note. However it is not his most serious criticism.

Also Christian, Nietzsche says, is

> mortal enmity against the lords of the earth, against the 'noble' – along with a sly, secret rivalry.... Christian, finally, is the hatred of the *spirit*, of pride, courage, freedom, liberty of the spirit....[5]

Here we find the Nietzschean theme of nobility and the noble virtues. Christianity rejects the noble virtues – not outrightly, but slyly – in favour of humility and the other virtues of weakness, chastity and poverty – in short, in favour of '*holiness*', which, for Nietzsche, does more harm to life than any vice.[6]

Christian, too, is opposition to the truth, or at least a lack of respect for the truth, which amounts to the same thing for Nietzsche. For Christianity

It is a matter of complete indifference whether something is true, while it is of the utmost importance whether it is believed to be true. Truth and the *faith* that something is true: two completely separate realms of interest – almost diametrically opposite realms....[7]

It is not merely that Christianity is indifferent to truth. In the theological elaboration of Christianity, Nietzsche finds a more serious opposition to truth.

Whatever a theologian feels to be true *must* be false: this is almost a criterion of truth. His most basic instinct of self-preservation forbids him to respect reality at any point or even to let it get a word in. Wherever the theologians' instinct extends *value judgments* have been stood on their heads and the concepts of 'true' and 'false' are of necessity reversed: whatever is most harmful to life is called 'true'; whatever elevates it, enhances, affirms, justifies it, and makes it triumphant, is called 'false'.[8]

Here we are closer to the bone. For Nietzsche, Christianity denies the natural instincts, which are directed toward strength. The 'theologians' instinct' denies and opposes the natural instincts of life – the basic, natural and life-enhancing instincts that tend toward strength – which 'the higher type of man' embraces. Christianity 'has placed all the basic instincts of this type [the higher type of man] under the ban; and out of these instincts it has distilled evil and the Evil One: the strong man as the typically reprehensible man....'[9] As Christianity has reversed 'true' and 'false', so it has reversed 'good' and 'bad', making 'good' what tends toward weakness.

For Nietzsche, if there is a primary instinct it is the instinct to gain power, the will to power. In *The Antichrist* he says,

What is good? Everything that heightens the feeling of power in man, the will to power, power itself.
What is bad? Everything that is born of weakness.[10]

It is not so much that power, or the will to power, is the chief virtue among the noble virtues; rather, it is the primary virtue that orders and gives form to the others. So it is that in *Beyond Good and Evil* Nietzsche says that the noble man out of a sense of power wants to give, wants to help the unfortunate, and, honouring himself as the powerful one, subjects himself to severity and hardness.[11] Christianity, by making power evil, makes evil what is our primary good and disorders all the noble virtues.

As a part of Nietzsche's attack is directed against the theologians, so a part of his attack, a more significant part, is directed against the priests, the devious priests.

> Decadence is only a *means* for the type of man who demands power in Judaism and Christianity, the *priestly* type: this type of man has a life interest in making mankind *sick* and in so twisting the concepts of good and evil, true and false, as to imperil life and slander the world.[12]

That the priests seek power cannot be bad, for Nietzsche; but they seek to gain power deviously, by teaching the virtues of weakness, and by making humankind sick. They twist values so severely as to reverse them. 'All the concepts of the church', says Nietzsche,

> have been recognized for what they are, the most malignant counterfeits that exist, the aim of which is to devalue nature and natural values…. [T]he concepts 'beyond,' 'Last Judgement,' 'immortality of the soul,' and 'soul' itself are instruments of torture, systems of cruelties by virtue of which the priest became master, remained master.[13]

At the same time, 'every natural custom, every natural institution' (Nietzsche mentions the 'state, judicial order, marriage, care of the sick and poor') and 'every demand inspired by the instinct of life – in short, everything that contains its value *in itself*' is devalued by the priests and given a new value which they create, no longer a natural value, understood in terms of 'disobedience of God, that is, of the priest'.[14]

Paul, for Nietzsche, exemplifies the priestly type. Paul the priest seeks and gains power through the use of 'concepts, doctrines, [and] symbols', such as the doctrines of immortality and the Last Judgement. Such doctrines, though he is too clever to believe them himself, Paul as priest uses to tyrannize and to manipulate the 'masses', and to form 'herds'; so Nietzsche judges Paul.[15] The success of the priestly effort to tyrannize the masses depends on such otherworldly doctrines. Kierkegaard too, as we have seen, is suspicious of an otherworldly faith, although his concern is different from Nietzsche's. In *Fear and Trembling* his, or Johannes', concern is that a faith and trust directed toward a future life deny trust in God now, in this life, and so this is not faith at all, but a form of despair. Also Kierkegaard, like Nietzsche, voiced criticism of the 'Established Church' and its clergy, as a part of his attack upon 'Christendom'. But he does not accuse 'official Christianity' of a devious mendacity designed to arrogate power to itself; rather, he accuses it of dishonestly mitigating the hard demands of faith.[16]

Nietzsche's primary criticism, we should be clear, is of Christianity, not of those he sees as its ignoble minions, the theologians and the priests, although, as we have seen, the theologians and priests take some fire. Much of his criticism of the theologians and priests he also applies to Christianity itself: hatred of the senses, twisting of values, indifference to the truth. The Christianity he was familiar with from the inside, the Lutheranism of his upbringing, was of course strongly influenced by the words of Paul, and most, if not all, of the animadversions we have noted are on Christianity after Paul. (As we shall see, Nietzsche has criticisms of Jesus that are different from his criticisms of the followers of Christianity.) When Nietzsche tries to provide 'a psychology of faith',[17] as he does, he has in mind especially the Christianity with which he is contemporaneous, a Christianity influenced by Paul. It is in Nietzsche's psychological probing of Christianity's hidden springs and feelings, to which we now turn, that we find his deepest criticisms of Christianity.

Like Kierkegaard, Nietzsche is a psychologist, but what he finds when he probes the hidden aspects of faith is very different from what Kierkegaard found. The Christian, for Nietzsche, is 'the herd animal, the sick human animal',[18] who fears and regards as evil those who are strong. What is the emotional response of the Christian to those who are strong? Is it love? Given what we have seen so far, it will not surprise us that Nietzsche finds 'at the bottom of Christianity' the rancour of the sick directed against what is healthy.[19] The secret emotion of Christianity for Nietzsche the psychologist is rancour. It is also through the lenses of his psychological reflection that Nietzsche discovers, or believes he discovers, the role of pity in Christianity. 'Christianity is called the religion of *pity'*, says Nietzsche – and rightly so he believes. What is pity? On Nietzsche's analysis, pity

> stands opposed to the tonic emotions which heighten our vitality: it has a depressing effect. We are deprived of our strength when we feel pity. The loss of strength which suffering as such inflicts on life is still further increased and multiplied by pity. Pity makes suffering contagious.[20]

Pity, felt toward the weak, encourages their weakness and preserves the weak in their weakness. But pity also makes weak those who feel pity. Thus, as Nietzsche says, pity multiplies weakness.

However, it is when he proposes the *motive* of Christian faith that Nietzsche the psychologist strikes deepest against Christianity. Anticipating Freud, Nietzsche sees that, in challenging religious belief, a more serious question than 'On what basis do you believe?' is 'What motivates you to believe?' In *Thus Spoke Zarathustra* he addresses this question as it relates to religious belief. There Nietzsche, through the persona of Zarathustra, proclaims: it is a 'weariness that does not want to want any more' that has 'created all gods and afterworlds'.[21] In *The Antichrist* Nietzsche is more elaborate. There, focusing on Christianity, he says: 'The fear of pain, even of infinitely minute pain – that can end in no other way than in a *religion of love*.'[22] And elsewhere in *The Antichrist* he avows that it is hatred of reality – of the world, we may say – that is the 'motivating force at the root of Christianity'.[23] Nietzsche is clear, then, that religious faith is not a spontaneous response to the Divine. It is motivated. The motives he proposes vary slightly: weariness, fear of pain, hatred of the world. But they all are joyless and spring from a spirit of rejection. And they all are hidden, hidden not only from those outside religion, but from religious believers themselves; the last to be aware of their motives for belief, for Nietzsche, are those whose faith is created by such motives.

In addition, for Nietzsche, overlaying this motivation of faith, is a further motive for the *morality* of Christianity. Nietzsche associates this motive with the teachings of Paul, whom he quotes, or paraphrases, to this effect:

> But God hath chosen the foolish things of the world to ruin the wise; and God hath chosen the weak things of the world to ruin

what is strong; and base things of the world; and things which
are despised, hath God chosen, yea, and what is nothing, to bring
to naught what is something: That no flesh should glory in his
presence.

Nietzsche immediately makes this comment:

> To understand this passage, a first-rate document for the psy-
> chology of every chandala morality, one should read the first
> inquiry in my *Genealogy of Morals*: there the contrast between a
> *noble* morality and a chandala morality, born of *ressentiment* and
> impotent vengefulness, was brought to light for the first time.
> Paul was the greatest of all apostles of vengeance.[24]

In *The Genealogy of Morals* (in Sec. 10 of the First Essay) the contrast
between a noble morality and a chandala morality, or what
Nietzsche there calls a 'slave morality', is that the first is un-
abashedly affirmative, while the second, created by *ressentiment*,
says 'no' to what is different or outside itself. The first is oriented
toward strength as a virtue, the second toward weakness as a
virtue. While there is more to the contrast between these two
morality types in Nietzsche's conception of them (as we shall see in
Chapter 7), we have seen enough for our present purposes. The
motive of a chandala morality, a slave morality, the morality of
Christianity or of Christianity after Paul, is the secret desire for
revenge – *ressentiment*. *Ressentiment* is not a forthright resentment
or an explicit desire for revenge: it is a secret desire for revenge
against one's betters, masked by overt but false expressions of
neighbourly love. 'The principle of "Christian love"', says
Nietzsche, is that 'in the end it wants to be *paid* well.'[25]
    In *The Antichrist*, then, Nietzsche the psychologist criticizes faith
by uncovering what, for him, are its hidden springs and inclina-
tions. Also, however, he recasts faith and its place in Christianity.
Let us see how Nietzsche does this. Referring to the faith of the
'glad tidings', Nietzsche says of such a faith that

> [i]t does not prove itself either by miracle or by reward and
> promise, least of all 'by scripture': at every moment it is its own
> miracle, its own reward, its own proof, its own 'kingdom of
> God.' Nor does this faith formulate itself: it *lives*, it resists all
> formulas.[26]

Here, interestingly, on *this* point there may be little disagreement between Nietzsche and Kierkegaard. For Kierkegaard too, always and especially in the *Postscript*, faith is not a matter of 'formulas', not a matter of 'objective belief', not a matter of simply holding to be true the true propositions of Christianity.

Again, Nietzsche is not seriously at odds with Kierkegaard when he says that the '"kingdom of heaven" is a state of the heart – not something that is to come "above the earth" or "after death"'.[27] While Kierkegaard may not have denied that there is personal immortality, for him faith is not for a future life, but for this life. Directed to a future existence it becomes a form of despair. In Nietzsche's recasting of faith, so far as these points go, there is no denial of faith, only a dismissal of what wrongly passes for faith: so Kierkegaard would allow. Nietzsche's renovations are not yet complete, however.

Interlacing with the comments on faith we have just noted we find this Nietzschean pronouncement:

> It is not 'faith' that distinguishes the Christian: the Christian *acts*, he is distinguished by acting *differently*: by not resisting, either in words or in his heart, those who treat him ill; by making no distinction between foreigner and native...; by not growing angry with anybody, by not despising anybody, by not permitting himself to be seen or involved in courts of law ('not swearing'); by not divorcing his wife under any circumstances....[28]

Continuing the same theme, Nietzsche says:

> I go back, I tell the *genuine* history of Christianity. The very word 'Christianity' is a misunderstanding: in truth there was only *one* Christian, and he died on the cross.... It is false to the point of nonsense to find the mark of the Christian in a 'faith', for instance, in the faith in redemption through Christ: only Christian *practice*, a life such as he *lived* who died on the cross is Christian.
>
> Not a faith, but a doing; above all a *not* doing of many things, another state of *being*.... To reduce being a Christian, Christianism, to a matter of considering something true, to a mere phenomenon of consciousness, is to negate Christianity. *In fact there have been no Christians at all.*[29]

What is Christian is not a faith, but a doing, above all a not-doing, says Nietzsche. He repeats this point several times in *The Antichrist*.

Much of what is not to be done by the Christian, for Nietzsche, is enumerated in what I quoted above. In another nearby passage Nietzsche says this about the practice of the Redeemer and the 'legacy' of 'the bringer of glad tidings': 'He does not resist, he does not defend his right, he takes no step which might ward off the worst; on the contrary, he *provokes* it.'[30]

This idea – practice, and not faith, is Christian – recasts faith so severely as to exclude it from Christian religiousness. And this idea is, to be sure, in opposition to Kierkegaard's thinking on faith. For Kierkegaard, being a Christian *is* a matter of having faith, and – as is inescapably clear in *Fear and Trembling* – while faith, as a passion, involves a 'doing', involves practice, it also is, and is more centrally, unwavering and certain trust in God. Still, Kierkegaard can agree that Christianity is not a matter of 'considering something true' and agree that it makes Christianity ludicrous to regard it so. He would only point out that Nietzsche is wrong to regard faith as essentially faith *that* some religious proposition is true, as he seems to do when he regards faith as 'for instance faith in redemption through Christ' – in spite of his earlier insistence that faith 'resists all formulas'. 'There have been no Christians at all,' says Nietzsche. Rather, for Johannes de Silentio, every second person may be a Christian, be a knight of faith. If every second person is a knight of faith, though, they are not knights by virtue of acknowledging right things to be true: despite all the members of Christendom with their habitual or social belief, Johannes can agree with Nietzsche, there may be no Christians at all.

Nietzsche, however, has one more turn of the screw. 'Not "repentance"', he says, 'not "prayer for forgiveness", are the ways to God: *only the evangelical practice* [the practice of the life of Christ] leads to God, indeed it *is* "God".'[31] So, finally for Nietzsche, God *is* practice. But this is a denial of God in any traditional sense. It denies a God who is a creator of all that is, a God to whose will one should try to conform one's own will, a God who offers love and forgiveness to His creatures. It denies a God in whom one has faith and with whom there can be a faith relationship of the sort Abraham is portrayed as having in *Fear and Trembling*.

Thus, in that part of his thinking in which he recasts faith, Nietzsche excludes faith from religion in two ways: first, by replacing faith with practice and, second, by reducing God to practice; On the other hand, for Nietzsche, if there is faith in a transcendent God, such a faith rests upon hidden desires and motives. Nietzsche in effect poses a dilemma in *The Antichrist*: either Christianity is Christian faith, faith in God, in which case it is false and rests on hidden motives; or it is practice to the exclusion of faith.

Clearly, for Nietzsche, it is better if Christianity is practice. However, Nietzsche is far from recommending the practice of Christianity, which is a practice of not-doing. Such practice is too nihilistic for him, the very opposite of a practice of the will to power. The word he applies to Jesus, the exemplar of this practice, is a word he takes from Dostoyevsky: the word 'idiot'.[32]

Nietzsche's criticism of Jesus is not that Jesus is directed by a secret desire for revenge. That is Nietzsche's criticism of the *followers* of Christianity, and Jesus is not a follower. In a way he is a creator of new values and, to the extent that he is, Nietzsche admires him. In fact Nietzsche exhibits an ambivalence toward Jesus. Nietzsche's ambivalence is fairly evident in *The Antichrist* and, I think, emerges in what I have presented. However, it is more obvious in the portrait of Jesus that Nietzsche gives us in *Thus Spoke Zarathustra*. In the Fourth Part of that work Zarathustra encounters in quick succession a number of 'higher men'. Each is a quasi-mythical, symbolic evocation of a type, and each is in some way higher than those who are trapped in the smallness of the common run of humanity. Yet each is in some way lacking. Among these higher men is one that Nietzsche labels 'the voluntary beggar', voluntary because he has given away his riches. While the voluntary beggar is not named, it is clear beyond a shadow of doubt that Nietzsche has in mind Jesus.

Zarathustra finds the voluntary beggar giving a sermon, a sermon on a knoll – and he is giving it to cows! His message, as he expresses it to Zarathustra, is this:

> Except we turn back and become as cows, we shall not enter the kingdom of heaven. For we ought to learn one thing from them: chewing the cud. And, verily, what would it profit a man if he gained the whole world and did not learn this one thing: chewing the cud! He would not get rid of his melancholy – his great melancholy; but today that is called *nausea*.[33]

The voluntary beggar has overcome his nausea, and that is no little thing for Nietzsche, for he associates nausea with that smallness of spirit that precludes true nobility. And what was it that nauseated the voluntary beggar? It was the rich, 'the gilded, false mob'.[34] But, he discovered, the poor were little better, for they too are motivated by 'lascivious greed, galled envy, aggrieved vengefulness'. There was no abiding difference between the rich and the poor, he found: both the rich and the poor follow the way of 'the mob'. So the voluntary beggar rejected the poor as well as the rich and fled yet farther, until he came to the cows and their pure contentment.

What are, for Nietzsche, strengths of the voluntary beggar are not difficult to identify. He has become aware of his nausea and overcome it. He rejects vengefulness, the secret desire for revenge. He rejects the values of 'the mob', and he consciously creates values in their place. He, following the cows, has rejected 'gravity'; and gravity, or 'the spirit of gravity', is one of Nietzsche's special demons (about which more later). And he is engaged in practice.

Equally evident are what for Nietzsche are the weaknesses of the voluntary beggar. While the voluntary beggar consciously creates values, he creates wrong values. He is a 'plant-and-root man', Zarathustra says. He is 'averse to the joys of the flesh' and he 'love[s] honey'. This is to say that he denies his natural instincts and is too attached to the softness of contentment. The main value he creates is chewing the cud – that is, a 'peacefulness' that Nietzsche satirizes as an unrelenting absent-mindedness. The voluntary beggar dismisses the aristocratic values of the noble and, at bottom, is an opponent of power and the will to power. The voluntary beggar is a parody of Christ and His teachings, but the teachings of Christ satirized by Nietzsche, and to which he objects, are clear enough: at the root of it all is what Nietzsche perceives to be a rejection of power and so of life itself. It emerges, then, that Nietzsche's criticism of Jesus and his practice is the same as his root criticism of Christianity and faith.

6

Zarathustra, the Prophet of the *Übermensch*, and the Death-of-God Theme

Nietzsche wrote *Thus Spoke Zarathustra* in the 1880s at the height of his powers. Each of the first three of the book's four parts he dashed off in about ten days.[1] It is a major work, at once an epic-like account of the moral trials that Zarathustra must endure and a collection of Zarathustra's prophetic speeches. In the manner of an allegory, it also contains Zarathustra's encounters with various other quasi-mythical symbolic figures. These other opposing figures – the saint, the soothsayer, the dwarf, who is the spirit of gravity, and others, including the various higher men – speak in dialogue with Zarathustra. In this way there is in *Thus Spoke Zarathustra*, though on a smaller scale, something like the polyphony that we find in Kierkegaard's pseudonymous corpus between his pseudonymous authors.

After ten years of solitude and reflection Zarathustra awakens one morning and, gazing upon the dawn, finds himself with the sense that it is time to share his wisdom – he decides to descend from his mountains to the inhabited valleys below. So begins *Thus Spoke Zarathustra*. The wisdom that he would share is the message of the *Übermensch*. He descends from his mountains to call upon humankind to become bridges to the *Übermensch*.

Zarathustra is a prophet, as we have had occasion to observe. As a prophet, he often communicates directly in his speeches and pronouncements; he is not restricted to indirect communication, as is Johannes de Silentio. This is so even though Nietzsche, as he unfolds Zarathustra's career, uses parables and symbolic visions – devices of indirect communication – to tell us the story of Zarathustra's trials and encounters.

Above all, Zarathustra is a prophet and he is the prophet of the *Übermensch* (since *Mensch* means man generically, or human being,

Nietzsche's category does not exclude women, despite the regret-
tably silly and even misogonystic things that Nietzsche says about
women here and there). In the first town he comes to, he announces
in the market-place: 'I teach you the [*Übermensch*]. Man is something that shall be overcome.'² But his message is not received.
'Behold, I am a herald of the lightning and a heavy drop from the
cloud; but this lightning is called [*Übermensch*].'³ But they do not
hear his message. The people in the market-place do not wish to
hear of overcoming; they wish to hear of happiness. Zarathustra
leaves the town reflecting that his wisdom is for the few. He will
not become 'the shepherd and dog of a herd'; his message is for
'the lonesome, and the twosome; and whoever still has ears for the
unheard-of'.⁴

So ends 'Zarathustra's Prologue'. Zarathustra will seek bridges
to the *Übermensch,* among the few who have ears, and to them he
directs his speeches. The people of the market-place are not ready
for his wisdom, Zarathustra has discovered; and, we may suppose,
Nietzsche had himself come to the same discovery. For his contemporaries – the people of the market-place of Europe – have not yet
assimilated the great Nietzschean truth that God is dead. In order
for the *Übermensch* to come, and in order for there to be an
Übermensch, it cannot be that God is the source of values. For
Nietzsche, of course, God is not the source of values, nor is there a
God. God from the beginning, for Nietzsche, was a myth; and the
old myth is dead. But, moreover, it is necessary that those who are
to be bridges to the *Übermensch* consciously reject God. The old
myth is dead culturally, but not all know this in the fibre of their
being. The death-of-God theme emerges early in *Thus Spoke
Zarathustra*. In the prologue, on his way to that first town,
Zarathustra meets the saint in the forest. The saint recognizes
Zarathustra, for years ago he had seen Zarathustra pass his way as
he journeyed to the mountains and their solitude. And he asks,
why does Zarathustra leave his solitude for the realm of men?
Zarathustra replies, 'I love man.' He would give them the gift of
his wisdom. The saint proclaims that he himself sought the solitude
of the forest because he 'loved man all-too-much'. 'Now', he says, 'I
love God; man I love not.' And he advises Zarathustra not to go to
men, but to return to his mountains. Zarathustra is not deterred,
but as he leaves the saint he muses: 'Could it be possible? This old
saint in the forest has not yet heard anything of this, that *God is
dead*.'⁵ The saint sequestered in the forest has not heard that God is

dead, but those in the market-place have, for they are not isolated from the cultural rejection of God. Yet they are like the saint in that they have not assimilated this truth.

The death of God is central to Nietzsche's thought, and the nuances in his development of this theme make his expression of it distinctly Nietzschean. However, Nietzsche is not the originator of the death-of-God theme. There are a number of nineteenth-century precedents. Hegel in 1802 had referred to '[the] feeling ... [of the] religion of modern times ... [that] God is dead'.[6] Heine, in his *On the History of Religion and Philosophy in Germany (Zur Geschicht der Religion und Philosophie in Deutschland)*, commenting on Kant's publication of his first *Critique*, wrote: 'Do you hear the little bell tinkle? Kneel down – one brings the sacraments for a dying God.' Nietzsche was not unacquainted with Heine's writings and may have read this passage.[7] Ernest Renan, in a work entitled *Prayer on the Acropolis*, which he published in 1876, reflected that 'gods die like men and it is not right that they should be eternal'.[8] True, he is speaking of 'gods' and not 'God' (the prayer is to Athena). But the idea of a deity dying is there. Nietzsche refers to Renan in *The Antichrist*, but he there has in mind Renan as the author of *The Life of Jesus*, and is only concerned to reject Renan's view of the character of Jesus. And of course there is Swinburne, the English Victorian poet, who in 1871 wrote 'Hymn of Man', in which he says of God that 'he was God, and is dead'. In the last lines of Swinburne's poem we find: 'Thou art smitten, thou God, thou art smitten; thy death is upon thee, O Lord'.[9] Here is the idea that *we* have 'smitten' God, which anticipates a turn that Nietzsche will give to the death-of-God theme. The idea of the death of God is abroad in the nineteenth century, it would seem. Indeed, it has been said that if God died, He died in the nineteenth century.

All of these authors refer to the death of God before Nietzsche does. Nevertheless it is Nietzsche who is most closely associated with the theme, and rightly so. For it is Nietzsche who most richly develops the theme, turning it several ways and integrating it into his thought. The death-of-God theme is not sounded by Nietzsche for the first time in *Thus Spoke Zarathustra*. Nietzsche gives it its most oracular statement in *The Gay Science (Die Fröhliche*

Wissenschaft), a work he published in 1882, the year before he began writing *Thus Spoke Zarathustra*. The passage deserves to be quoted at some length:

> *The Madman.* Have you not heard of that madman who lit a lantern in the bright morning hours, ran to the market place, and cried incessantly, 'I seek God! I seek God!' As many of those who did not believe in God were standing around just then, he provoked much laughter. Has he got lost? asked one. Did he lose his way like a child? asked another. Or is he hiding? Is he afraid of us? Has he gone on a voyage? or emigrated? Thus they yelled and laughed.
>
> The madman jumped into their midst and pierced them with his eyes. 'Whither is God?' he cried. 'I shall tell you. We *have killed him* – you and I. All of us are his murderers. But how did we do this? How could we drink up the sea? Who gave us the sponge to wipe away the entire horizon? What were we doing when we unchained the earth from its sun? Whither is it moving now? Whither are we moving? Away from all suns? Are we not plunging continually? Backward, sideward, forward, in all directions? Is there any up or down left? ... Do we hear nothing as yet of the noise of the gravediggers who are burying God? Do we smell nothing as yet of the divine decomposition? Gods, too, decompose. God is dead. God remains dead. And we have killed him.
>
> 'How shall we comfort ourselves, the murderers of all murderers? What was holiest and mightiest of all that the world has yet owned has bled to death under our knives.... . Is not the greatness of this deed too great for us? Must we ourselves not become gods simply to appear worthy of it? ...'
>
> Here the madman fell silent and looked again at his listeners; and they, too, were silent and stared at him in astonishment. At last he threw his lantern on the ground, and it broke into pieces and went out. 'I have come too early,' he said then; 'my time is not yet. This tremendous event is still on its way, still wandering; it has not yet reached the ears of men. Lightning and thunder require time; the light of the stars requires time; deeds, though done, still require time to be seen and heard. This deed is still more distant from them than the most distant stars – *and yet they have done it themselves.*'[10]

Clearly, Nietzsche's madman prefigures Zarathustra. As Zarathustra is a prophet, the madman is a seer, and he, like

Zarathustra in the prologue, speaks to the people of the market-place. However, in his madman aphorism Nietzsche allows himself a thicker overlay of allusion. The madman is a Diogenes seeking God with his lantern in the brightness of day. Like Diogenes, he knew what he would find. When the unbelievers of the market-place mock the madman they ironically echo Elijah's mocking of the priests of Ba'al when Ba'al does not respond to their invocation (1 Kings 18:27). Though the madman says, 'I seek God!' he of course knows just what he is doing 'seeking' God. The townspeople are prepared to ridicule his apparent belief that there is a God to find, but they fall silent when he tells them that they, and he, have killed God.

The death-of-God theme, as Nietzsche uses it, contains several strata. At one level it means that the myth of God is dead, that it can no longer be believed that there is a God. So it is that Nietzsche says elsewhere in *The Gay Science* that 'the greatest recent event – that "God is dead", that belief in the Christian god has become un-believable – is already beginning to cast its first shadows over Europe'.[11] The townspeople in the market-place, or some of them, do not believe in God; they have come this far. More than that the myth is dead in the sense that it is unbelievable, the theme implies that there is no God: God does not exist, which further implies that God never did exist. But while the non-existence of God is a stratum of the theme, more than that God does not and never did exist is contained in the death-of-God theme. A non-existence claim can be made about islands and planets, and God is not like an island or planet. God, in the religious tradition that Nietzsche is ad-dressing, is a living God. Only a living God can die, only a God that has animated lives and given them direction and substance can die. Part of the import of Nietzsche's theme is that the God who provided moral direction and significance for our lives can no longer play this role. The story of this God no longer engages us at a deep enough psychological level to play this role, and so in this sense, too, God is dead.

All of the strata of the death-of-God theme identified in the last paragraph, it should be noted, are passive. They indicate a state that God is in – non-existence – or something that has happened to our belief in God or something that has happened to the power of the story of God to engage our lives. But in the madman aphorism a signal stratum of the theme is that God's dying is not an event that happened, descending upon us, as it were: it is an event that we have brought about – we have killed God. There is something we did and are doing to outgrow the old myth and to alienate the story from any engagement with our lives. Nietzsche perceives that it is this element of the death-of-God theme that is most difficult fully to internalize. When the madman announces to the townspeople that they, and he, have killed God, they cease laughing and fall silent. It is one thing to find the belief in God to be dead, unbelievable; it is another to take responsibility for having brought this about. Yet, for Nietzsche, this element – that the death of God is our doing – must be accepted in order for the death of God to be accepted in its full significance. Nietzsche returns to this subtheme in *Thus Spoke Zarathustra*, where he develops it with an amazing delicacy and power, along with other versions of the main death-of-God theme.

As we have seen, the death-of-God theme is presented early in *Thus Spoke Zarathustra*. It recurs in Zarathustra's speeches in each of the four parts of the work. However, Nietzsche reserves his most sustained development of the theme in its variations until the fourth and last part of *Zarathustra*, where the theme is integral to the character of two of the 'higher men' encountered by Zarathustra.

The first is the retired pope.[12] God is dead, and the last pope has 'retired'. When Zarathustra encounters him he 'has lost his way' and asks for help. He explains that he was seeking 'the last pious man', the saint – the same saint that Zarathustra had met in the prologue – in the hope that he would not yet have heard 'what all the world knows today', that God is dead. However, he tells Zarathustra sadly, he did not find the saint in his cave, for the saint is dead. He had been hoping to have one more religious festival, 'a festival of pious memories and divine services'. And then he says something curious: since the most pious of believers is dead he has resolved to seek 'the most pious of all those who do not believe in God – ... Zarathustra'. To this point the old pope was not aware of the identity of the one to whom he was speaking, but now Zarathustra identifies himself. And, Zarathustra asks, is it true that God died of pity, 'that pity strangled him'? The retired pope confirms this and, in accord with themes in *The Antichrist*, says, 'When he was young, this god out of the Orient ... was harsh and vengeful ... [e]ventually, however, he became old and soft and mellow and pitying [until finally] he sat in his nook by the hearth, wilted, grieving over his weak legs, weary of the world, weary of

willing, and one day choked on his all-too-great pity.' Pity spreads
the contagion of weakness and makes the one who pities weak:
God has grown so weak from his pity that he has died of it.

One way Nietzsche turns the death-of-God theme is by varying
the kind of death that God has suffered. In this exchange between
Zarathustra and the old pope Nietzsche allows that God has died of
pity – a variant on the death-of-God theme that he had presented
earlier, in the second part of *Thus Spoke Zarathustra*, where
Zarathustra says that the devil once told him: 'God is dead; God
died of his pity for man.'[13] When the old pope in effect confirms
this, Zarathustra muses, 'When gods die, they always die several
kinds of death.'[14] In another variant, again offered earlier, the gods
laughed themselves to death. 'That happened', says Zarathustra,
'when the most godless word issued from one of the gods themselves – "There is one god. Thou shalt have no other god before
me!"' At this, says Zarathustra, 'all the gods laughed and rocked on
their chairs' – until they died from laughing.[15]

In any case, however God died, from Nietzsche's standpoint it is
a strength of the old pope that he clearly recognizes the death of
God. But this 'higher man' also has his flaws. While for
Zarathustra, and Nietzsche, the death of God is a great event, for
the last pope it is an occasion for sadness and melancholy. He con-
cedes that God is dead but wishes it were otherwise. He is nostalgic
for the old times and so seeks the saint in the hope he has not yet
heard the prodigious news. Perhaps, he hopes, he can have a religious festival after all. He hankers after religious piety, and if the
piety of belief is lost to him he will turn to the godless piety of
Zarasthustra. The old pope is far from feeling the right way about
the death of God, and, of course, he is further yet from acknowledging that he has killed God. For Nietzsche, there are miles to go
after one has acknowledged God's death.

Of the 'higher men' that Zarathustra encounters, there is one
other for whose character the death-of-God theme is integral. He is
'the ugliest man'.[16] Moreover, in the case of the ugliest man the
theme takes the form of killing God, the subtheme that emerges in
the madman aphorism of *The Gay Science*. The ugliest man is the
self-confessed murderer of God. He does not deny his deed –
unlike the townspeople in *The Gay Science*. But he is grotesquely
ugly. Zarathustra is seized by pity for him, but only for a moment.
He immediately overcomes his pity. Zarathustra's more enduring
feeling is shame; he feels ashamed for the ugliest man.

Why is the ugliest man ugly? And why does Zarathustra feel ashamed for him? Has he not killed God and done so with a fully conscious intent? He has indeed killed God, but he has done so out of revenge. He has killed God because God had seen into all the dirty recesses of his life. This, and God's pity, he could not stand. And so he has taken *'revenge against the witness'*,[17] against the omniscient witness. The ugliest man acknowledges that he is the murderer of God, but he feels dirty, ugly. He despises himself. He has not yet claimed his own act as a glorious act that opens the way to self-affirmation, the conscious and self-confident creation of new values, and the will to power.

It is not all that easy to allow that God is dead in the sense that the myth is no longer believable. For to allow only this, to cease to believe in God, is to deny that God is the source of our values. But, Nietzsche is clear, fully to accept the death of God is to accept that event as our own doing. Even that is not enough. Fully to accept the death of God is to accept this 'tremendous event' as our own deed, but *in the right way*, for it is possible to acknowledge it as our deed and to accept our deed in the wrong way, as the ugliest man has done.

The ugliest man, like the other higher men, is invited by Zarathustra to his cave. There they all gather, and Zarathustra speaks to them about what they must do to be truly 'higher'. At one point, while his guests are talking noisily, Zarathustra leaves the assembly in his cave. Outside he reflects upon their potential: amid some ambivalence, he feels a sense of optimism for their development. Just then, however, he realizes that the gay talk within the cave has given way to a strange silence. Zarathustra re-enters the cave to find the higher men on their knees, sunk in prayer. One of the higher men, one of the two kings, had been riding an ass, and in Zarathustra's brief absence the higher men had set up the ass as their god. Zarathustra discovers them adoring and praying to this, their new god. They have reverted to belief – to 'religious' belief in the ass. Zarathustra leaps among them and tries to pull them to their feet.

'Better to adore God in this form than in no form at all!' says the old pope. 'The old god lives again', says another higher man. 'In the case of gods death is always a mere prejudice', he asserts.[18] And, he says, it is the ugliest man who has awakened God again. So here we see what follows from the ugliest man accepting his deed in the wrong way. He has killed God, but in the wrong way, from the wrong motive, and he feels the wrong way about his deed. He has not dispelled the shadow of God. 'After Buddha was dead,' Nietzsche says in *The Gay Science*, 'his shadow was still shown for centuries in a cave – a tremendous, gruesome shadow. God is dead; but given the ways of men, there may still be caves for thousands of years in which his shadow will be shown.'[19] One of those caves, it turns out, is Zarathustra's own. The ugliest man has killed God, but he has not done so thoroughly, for he has not fully accepted his deed as a glorious accomplishment.

Nietzsche sees that we can in a sense know that God is dead while regarding God's death as something remote, a passive event peripheral to our lives. He sees that as a next step we can recognize that God is dead and see the relevance for our lives of this event, but find the death of God frightening, for we sense that the values that inform our lives are no longer moored. Beyond this, Nietzsche sees a further step: we must accept the death of God as our own act. But our acceptance of our act can still be of the wrong order. What is needed, for Nietzsche, is our seeing the event as our act *and* internalizing it as our own great and liberating accomplishment. For otherwise the old God may revive.

For Nietzsche, God and the *Übermensch* are exclusive. They are in opposition philosophically and psychologically, so that to allow the one is to deny the other. 'Dead are all gods', Zarathustra proclaims; 'now we want the [*Übermensch*] to live'.[20] All the gods – and this includes God, for Nietzsche – *must* be dead, or else the *Übermensch* cannot come. The *Übermensch* is a creator of new values and new meaning. Nietzsche sees that if there is a God, then there is no human creation of value or meaning.[21] By extension, if one believes in God, then one will not believe in the human creation of value; and of course one will not undertake consciously to create new values. If, on the other hand, there is no God we must 'become gods', as the madman says, in order to create new values to replace the old. Since God *is* dead, the task we must face in order to give ourselves new values is just the godlike task of creation. And this is frightening, so frightening that it cause 'apostasy', a return to faith, as happened in the case of the higher men. (Nietzsche calls 'apostates' those who become pious again – as they are from his perspective.)[22] For Nietzsche, it is not just that God and the *Übermensch* are exclusive; for Nietzsche, the *Übermensch* can *replace* God. 'Once one said God when one looked upon distant seas; but now', says Zarathustra, 'I have taught you to say: [*Übermensch*].'[23] However, there remains an insurmountable difference. While human beings created the myth of God, they cannot create a god; but they *can*, through their willing to be bridges, create the *Übermensch*.[24]

What we see is that Nietzsche is not a mere atheist. He is not interested in the merely metaphysical assertion that God does not exist. His rejection of God is fully religious. For Nietzsche, the death of God extends far beyond propositional belief to our behavioural proclivities, to our sensibility toward the world and toward one another, and – significantly – to what our values are and how we conceive those values. His vision of life's meaning, or the potential meaning we can give to life, he realized, is at odds with religion, faith and God at every level. For the *Übermensch* to come, for his vision to be realized – for human beings to become conscious creators of their values and meaning – he saw that God must die at even the deepest psychological level.

7

Transvaluation

If I was right in the last chapter, there is a tight symmetry in Nietzsche's thinking about God and value. If there is no God, we create our values; if we create our values, there is no God. It is a corollary of these Nietzschean propositions that, if there is a God, we do not create our values. For Nietzsche, if there were a God, then we would not be the creators of our values, for God and only God would be the source of value. Nietzsche, however, is clear that there is no God and that our values are just our human creation. Without that human creation we would have no values: we would have no moral values and our lives would have no value or meaning. For Nietzsche, as I have suggested, it is indeed in our power to create values, and this in itself, for Nietzsche, shows that there is no God. Nietzsche, let us observe, is not saying that we human beings *ought* to create our values. If this were the Nietzschean point it would allow that we might have failed to do what we ought to do – and this would allow that our existing values might not be our own creation. Rather, for him, our creation is the only source of values.[1] That is, *human* creation is the only source of values. Nietzsche allows that one person, or class of persons, can create values for others. This, for Nietzsche, is just what has happened in Christianity (as we saw in Chapter 5). The priests create values for others, the followers of Christianity, notably the value of obedience to the priestly will. These values are then imbibed by the followers of Christianity and assented to (this, for Nietzsche, being their unconscious creation of these values as values for themselves). Part of Nietzsche's objection to the values of the priests, and of religion, we will recall, is that these values devalue what is natural. However, setting aside this objection for the moment, for Nietzsche, such a state of affairs – some persons creating values for others – is not healthy in itself. Reflecting on Kant's categorical imperative as a universal test for morality, Nietzsche says that 'a virtue must be *our own* invention' and that 'the fundamental laws of self-preservation and growth demand ...

that everyone invent *his own* virtue'.[2] So Nietzsche allows that others can create values for us, but he argues that we as individuals should forthrightly create our own values. And in order to do so we must consciously create our values. In order to 'become gods', as the madman in *The Gay Science* would have us do, we must undertake *consciously* to create new values to replace the old. When Nietzsche in *Beyond Good and Evil* praises the noble individual as a creator of values, he is praising the noble individual's *conscious* creation of *his own* values: 'the noble type regards *himself* as a determiner of values ... he knows that it is he himself only who confers honour on things [by his creation]'.[3] For Nietzsche, as there is no God, we must strive to become as gods, we must become conscious creators of whatever new values we shall come to have – and if we do not undertake this erstwhile divine activity we shall not be free of the moribund values foisted upon us by the religion of the God who died.

Nietzsche in *The Antichrist*, as we have seen, thought of Christianity in its original form as a religion of not-doing. This suggests that for Nietzsche Christianity is a religion of negative values expressed as 'thou shalt not ...'. And this suggests in turn that for Nietzsche, if God is dead, and religious values are cast aside, then the constraints of morality will be loosened. In this connection one perhaps inevitably thinks of Ivan Karamazov's reflections. For Ivan, if there is no belief in immortality, then 'everything is permitted'.[4] Ivan, strictly, is reflecting on the constraining power of the belief in immortality; however the belief in immortality, for Ivan, is connected to belief in God.[5] If there is no belief in God, then there will be no belief in immortality; and so if the belief in God dies, 'everything is permitted'. So runs Ivan Karamazov's logic. Nietzsche's thinking is quite different, as Camus observed in *The Rebel*. For Ivan, as Camus sees it, if God is dead, 'everything is permitted'; for Nietzsche, if God is dead, 'nothing is permitted'.[6] In Nietzsche's view the values of Christianity, as they were originally taught by Jesus, 'devalued' nature. However, if these values are wiped away with the death of God, what remains is not moral permission to do what was lately forbidden, but a moral vacuum. In order for anything to be permitted, a new value must be created which makes that thing permissible. Camus so far is right. Going beyond Camus's point, let us observe that it is just as much a part of Nietzsche's thinking that nothing is forbidden if God is dead. If God is dead, then, until new values are created, nothing is permitted *and* nothing is forbidden. Human creation of new values will confer on goals, dispositions and actions, their goodness or badness, their obligatoriness or allowability.

This theme – that the value of life and all moral values, positive and negative, flow from human creation – I take to be an important strain of Nietzsche's moral thinking, one which runs right through much of his writing. This theme, or subtheme, is an integral part of his general theme of transvaluation. Of course, it is not all of his moral view. In addition, he denies that there are transcendent or universal values, as we saw in his objection to Kant. Any goods posited as 'universally valid' are, he says, 'chimeras'.[7] And there is another important theme, or subtheme, of Nietzsche's thinking about transvaluation: the theme of natural values.

It is in connection with this theme that Nietzsche speaks of power, the values of nature, and noble virtues. In *The Antichrist*, as we have seen (Chapter 5), he says:

> What is good? Everything that heightens the feeling of power in man, the will to power, power itself.
> What is bad? Everything that is born of weakness.

In the same way Zarathustra speaks of power as a 'new virtue' and a 'new good and evil'.[8] All of this makes it sound as though power, or the will to power, is the very *standard* for the good, a standard against which we can measure the values created by individuals. If so, then power is an underlying value that exists naturally and thus independently of human creation.

For that matter, what of the other natural or noble values that Nietzsche mentions, such as courage and pride? Even as Zarathustra urges the 'higher men' to be creators for themselves he exhorts them to have courage and pride.[9] These, it seems, are virtues that they *ought* to create for themselves. In fact, Nietzsche, through the voice of Zarathustra and in other writings, provides us with what amounts to a list of natural values and noble virtues that we should have. These are some of them: in addition to courage and pride, Zarathustra in his speech to the higher men urges them to have honesty, and self-reliance ('use your own legs'), to be creators for themselves, to have devotion to their 'work' ('your work, your will, that is *your* "neighbor"'), and more.[10] In *Beyond Good and Evil* Nietzsche presents as 'noble' some of these same attributes in a different formulation, as well as what may be some others: self-glorification, generosity that is 'giving and bestowing ... from an impulse generated by the super-abundance of power', 'reverence for all that is severe and hard', 'pride in oneself', but also 'faith in oneself' and 'enmity and irony towards "selflessness"'.[11] Zarathustra in another part of *Thus Spoke Zarathustra* affirms as a virtue selfishness, 'the wholesome, healthy selfishness that wells from a powerful soul'.[12] And, of course, given Nietzsche's condemnation of Christian asceticism and what he sees as Christianity's renunciation of the pleasures of the senses, he would affirm joy in the senses as a natural value.[13] Not just the will to power, but all of these values are natural, in Nietzsche's thinking, and so, not dependent upon human creation, it would seem.

In short, there is in Nietzsche's moral thought an internal tension between the two themes we have identified – the theme of the creation of value and the theme of natural value. It expresses itself as a problem that we may formulate as follows:

> If all values are created through human invention, then there are no discoverable values that exist independently of our creation. If there are natural values, then some values are discoverable and exist independently of human creation. Nietzsche seems to want it both ways.

These questions now come to the fore: Is power a universal? Are natural values universals? Can one honestly and consciously create as a value not seeking power for Nietzsche? If not, why not? Are there values that one should create, for Nietzsche? If so, do they not already exist as values?

However, it seems to me that Nietzsche can resolve this difficulty and adequately answer these questions. Here is the resolution to his problem that I would propose. Nietzsche can say that all values are created, but natural values are created in accord with our natural instincts and so are natural in the sense that they are not life-denying. Pre-eminent among such values is the will to power. Nevertheless, even the will to power is not a value for an individual until that individual wills it to be a value and so creates it as a value for himself or herself.

This resolution is consistent with Nietzsche's idea that the will to power is involved in all of life. Zarathustra says, 'where I found the living, there I found will to power'.[14] Still, some see a further problem having to do with the will to power. Robert Solomon observes:

> Nietzsche claims that all values and all actions are based upon the will to power. But then what is his ethics? If we do in fact act according to the will to power, it is pointless to tell us we *ought* to act accordingly....
> ...If we do (psychologically) necessarily act according to the will to power, it makes no sense to formulate an ethics which urges us to do so....[15]

Solomon argues on Nietzsche's behalf that, though for Nietzsche all values and all actions are based on the will to power, still, there may be various wrong conceptions of morality that do not recognize this fact. If this were the case, while there would be no sense in urging us to act in accord with the will to power, still there would be a point to Nietzsche's urging that we ought to recognize the underlying role that the will to power has. It seems to me that Nietzsche did believe that some moralities wrongly deny the place of the will to power in life, and so Solomon's comments are helpful in explaining Nietzsche's undertaking as he saw it. I would, however, amend one point that Solomon makes. While he is right that, for Nietzsche, the will to power exists where life exists, Nietzsche did not think that all posited or created values are *based* on power. Though he believed that power is basic to life, he saw that some moralities seek to negate, make evil, the will to power in others (as, for Nietzsche, the priests do in the Christian values they posit for others); and, Nietzsche thought, some consciously seek to negate, make evil, the will to power in themselves (as in original Christianity and in the message of Jesus, as Nietzsche saw it). Thus Nietzsche could consistently urge us to recognize the underlying role of the will to power in our lives and, furthermore, could consistently urge us to create the will to power as the chief virtue in our lives and to create as virtues in our lives the various other noble virtues, such as pride and courage.

Is the will to power, then, a universal for Nietzsche? It is universally present in all life, on Nietzsche's view, though he is aware that some deny its presence in their lives. It is, for him, a kind of *natural* universal – something like our physiological need for water, which also is a natural universal. The latter is a natural universal, given our physiological makeup; the former is a natural universal, given our psychological makeup, Nietzsche the psychologist believes he has discovered. But, for Nietzsche, from the will to power being a natural universal it does not follow that it is a *moral* universal, and it is to the positing of moral universals that Nietzsche objects, as in the case of Kant's ethics. The will to power will be a moral universal on Nietzsche's view, not by virtue of its being posited as such by some one person, Kant or anyone else but only if *all* will it as a value in their lives. This he exhorts us to do in our individual lives, though he is keenly aware that many are far from doing so.

Is the will to power a good? Nietzsche says that it is. For Nietzsche on my reading, we have a natural instinct toward power and the will to power, which makes it a need-fulfilling or natural good, just as water is, given our physiological needs. So, in order to be healthy and honest with ourselves, we *ought* to will it as our action-directing moral good. We cannot honestly deny the will to power in our lives, on Nietzsche's view, in the straightforward sense that in doing so we would dishonestly deny what is true, and what we at some level know to be true, about ourselves. But, again, on my reading of Nietzsche, the will to power will not be a *moral* good until we create it as a value by our willing it as such.

I believe that the foregoing is true to Nietzsche's thinking and that it adequately and consistently resolves the tension between the two moral themes he champions. Still, a bit more might be said about how Nietzsche understood our individual creation of value. Nietzsche excoriates Christian love, for he regards it as dishonest and full of *ressentiment*. But he does not therefore renounce love. Zarathustra speaks of a 'gift-giving love', which 'pile[s] up all the riches in [one's] soul', but only in order to give them as gifts of love – perhaps as Zarathustra himself is portrayed as doing. Such a love Zarathustra calls a 'whole and healthy...selfishness'.[16] Zarathustra goes on to speak of a 'great love' that overcomes both forgiveness and pity: 'if you have a suffering friend,' he says, 'be a resting place for his suffering, but a hard bed as it were, a field cot: thus will you profit him best'. Zarathustra proclaims: '"Myself I sacrifice to my love, *and my neighbor as myself*" – thus runs the speech of all creators. But all creators are hard.'[17]

What we see, then, is that for Nietzsche individual creation plays a role in determining the *form* of love that is to be a value, and so too for the other virtues, such as generosity. The point to be noted here, of course, is not that for Nietzsche Christian love is not a created value. Both Christian love and 'gift-giving love' are created by human invention, Nietzsche would insist. However, for Nietzsche, of the two only the second is a natural value, for only it is created to be in accord with our instincts and the severity that the will to power demands.

In the light of these considerations, and the resolution provided above, I think that we must allow Nietzsche can consistently hold all values are humanly created and yet speak of the will to power as a natural value – and can even go on to give us a list of subsidiary natural values and noble virtues. The resolution that I proposed does, I believe, accommodate very much if not all of what Nietzsche says about the creation of value and about the will to power and other natural values. Are there other possible resolutions more or less in accord with Nietzsche's views on morality? Arguably there are. One might interpret Nietzsche as saying that the will to power is a natural value in the strong sense that it is a value by virtue of our nature, and is *not* made a value by human creativity. This interpretation would be in accord with a fairly straightforward reading of the passage in *The Antichrist* where Nietzsche asks 'What is good?' and replies, 'the will to power, power'. Nietzsche, on this reading, is affirming power or the will to power as a logically prior standard for what is moral – that is, a discoverable moral standard that is prior to human decisions about what is of value. On this interpretation, not all values are created, although most might be. Are the other natural values created or pre-existing? Here I think the interpretation we are contemplating might answer either way. It might answer that, except for the will to power itself, the natural values, like those other values that devalue nature, are created by human invention; or it might answer that the will to power, as the standard for morality, entails the other natural values independently of any human invention, although the values that devalue nature are created by human invention. Given this bifurcation, we end up with at least three possible resolutions of the tension in Nietzsche's moral view. While I favour the one I proposed at first, I would allow that the other two can, with some Procrustean shaving, be made to fit Nietzsche's thinking. It remains that there is a way – at least one way – to resolve the tension in Nietzsche's moral view taken as a whole.

We should allow, then, that Nietzsche's moral views can be made consistent. Further, if we follow the resolution that I first proposed (to which I now revert), we may regard Nietzsche as being true to his moral vision when he holds both that there are natural values and that we ought to create these natural values and noble virtues for ourselves. And in the same way he is in accord with his moral thinking when he urges us to become 'annihilator[s] and break values': any who would be creators of new values must first destroy the old values, Zarathustra says.[18]

Summed up, Nietzsche's transvaluation theme, expressed as a Nietzschean exhortation, is this: the natural values of the earth must be embraced, they must be chosen by us as values through each individual's creation of them as values for himself or herself; we must affirm our natural instincts – the most basic of which is our will to power; the old religious, life-denying values must be rejected, and along with them the false transcendent and universal values that some would propose in their place; we must break the old tablets and create new tablets with new values that give new meaning to the earth.

Given this understanding of Nietzsche's transvaluation theme, we can see that Nietzsche is not a moral relativist. That is, he is not the kind of moral relativist that denies any morally relevant basis on which different sets of moral values can be judged. In this way he differs from Sartre, who may well have ended up with this kind of moral relativism.[19] Nietzsche would have been committed to such a moral relativism if he had embraced the theme of the human creation of values to the exclusion of the second theme of natural values. But this, I have argued, he does not do. As Kierkegaard in *Fear and Trembling* avoids a relativization of ethics$_2$, so Nietzsche avoids moral relativity. Nietzsche and Kierkegaard are alike in another way too regarding their respective approaches to morality. Each is critical of the way morality is understood in society. I do not mean that either is a social reformer: neither argues for, say, a new understanding of the requirements of social justice for the economically deprived – although Kierkegaard, in his non-pseudonymous *Works of Love*, does in effect try to bring out the deeper moral demands of love in our individual lives.[20] I mean that Nietzsche and Kierkegaard are alike in that both criticize the socially accepted understanding of the nature of 'ethics'. For both there is a higher ethics. But here all similarity ends. For Nietzsche, the higher ethics is a noble morality, comprised of values consciously created by those who have rejected the old life-denying values. For Kierkegaard, or Johannes de Silentio, it is an ethics whose overriding duties flow from an individual relationship to God.

8

Eternal Recurrence and Joyful Acceptance

Finally we come to Zarathustra's, and Nietzsche's, joyful acceptance. In the preceding several chapters we have put in place the background against which we must silhouette Nietzsche's acceptance if we are to perceive its distinctive form. Now we may draw it in against that backdrop. What Nietzsche evokes in *Thus Spoke Zarathustra* is not merely an image or conception of joyful acceptance; he evokes a movement in the interior of a human life, the life of Nietzsche's *alter ego*, Zarathustra, that expresses his conception. Important for Nietzsche's conception, or for his evocation of it, is Zarathustra's endurance of a moral trial. Interlaced with Zarathustra's speeches in *Thus Spoke Zarathustra* are Zarathustra's encounters with others, his journeys – and his two trials. As Abraham in *Fear and Trembling* underwent a trial of faith, so Zarathustra undergoes two moral trials. Each of his trials is of some importance for Zarathustra's character and for Nietzsche's message. Moreover the two trials he must undergo are connected. But one of them is particularly relevant to our concern in that the full character of Zarathustra's joyful acceptance emerges as we follow him through the ordeal of that trial. From it he issues joyful in his acceptance of all that is. The other trial, which is less relevant to our present concern, is the trial of pity. We have noted Nietzsche's diagnosis of the ailment of pity in *The Antichrist*. Yet Nietzsche saw that pity was a temptation even for those who are strong. It is a temptation for Zarathustra in particular, especially in the form of pity for the higher men. Zarathustra is not tempted to pity the lowly, but the higher men, with their flawed strength, bring him to the edge of pity (as we saw in the brief account in Chapter 6 of Zarathustra's meeting with the ugliest man). The trial of pity, suffice it to say for the present, Zarathustra overcomes. It is Zarathustra's other trial, and his overcoming of it, to which we must turn our attention.

Zarathustra's second trial is the trial of nausea. Both it and the trial of pity are, as it were, heard from offstage in much of *Thus Spoke Zarathustra*, although in places they come centre stage. The trial of pity is presented mainly in the Fourth Part, the part in which Zarathustra encounters the higher men. His trial of nausea – and his overcoming nausea – form a discernible, though intermittent, thread that runs from the Second Part right through to the end. When Nietzsche presents Zarathustra's trial of nausea he does so through the device of a premonition Zarathustra has – a dream or vision which presents Zarathustra with a riddle. In his vision Zarathustra sees himself standing among wild cliffs in bleak moonlight. Then he sees a man, a young shepherd, lying on the ground. A dog howls over him. The shepherd is gagging and writhing, his face distorted: from his mouth hangs the body of a snake. A large black snake had crawled into his mouth while he slept and bitten fast to his throat. Never has Zarathustra seen such dread and nausea on a face. He tries to pull the snake out of the shepherd's mouth, but he cannot. Then, on impulse, Zarathustra cries, 'Bite! Bite its head off! Bite!' And the shepherd does bite with a good bite. He spews out the head and jumps up. No longer a shepherd, no longer human, he is trans-formed – radiant and laughing with a laughter beyond any that Zarathustra has heard. So runs Zarathustra's vision. His vision is a parable, Zarathustra recognizes. 'What did I see…?' he asks. 'And who is it who must yet come one day?' 'Who is the shepherd?' 'Who is the man into whose throat all that is heaviest and blackest will crawl thus?'[1] And, we may also ask, what is this snake, this sum of all that is heaviest and blackest?

Nietzsche presents Zarathustra's vision in the Third Part of *Thus Spoke Zarathustra*. Later in the same part, in a section (or chapter) entitled 'The Convalescent', Zarathustra is depicted undergoing an actual trial. Back at his cave, sickened by nausea, he 'f[alls] down as one dead' and remains so for seven days. After seven days he arises. His trial is over. Zarathustra then explicates the parable of his vision. He, Zarathustra, was the shepherd. What he had seen in his vision was his own trial of nausea, and his triumph over nausea. And what was the snake, that which choked him with nausea? It was Zarathustra's great disgust with 'man' (*der Mensch*), with the smallness of man, with the smallness of man's best – and with the eternal recurrence of even the smallest.[2]

We have seen enough of Nietzsche's reflections in earlier chap-ters to appreciate why the smallness of man would disgust his *alter ego*, Zarathustra – in his smallness man cannot accept respons-ibility for the death of God, cannot become a creator of values and cannot embrace his own natural will to power. But Zarathustra's trial of nausea has much to do with accepting the *eternal recurrence* of the smallness of man. So it is that in order to understand what nauseates Zarathustra, and what finally he accepts joyfully, we must understand the Nietzschean category of eternal recurrence. In *Thus Spoke Zarathustra* the theme first emerges in an episode that immediately precedes Zarathustra's telling of his vision. In that episode Zarathustra has encountered the dwarf who is the spirit of gravity, his old opponent, and Zarathustra resolves to express to him his 'abysmal thought'. There is a gateway before them, and Zarathustra invites the dwarf to behold the two paths that meet there. One lane stretches backward for an eternity. The other stretches forward for an eternity. The gateway where they meet is inscribed 'Moment'. In the eternal lane that leads back-ward, 'Must not whatever *can* happen have happened?' asks Zarathustra. And in the eternal lane that leads forward, 'in this long dreadful lane – must we not eternally return?' Zarathustra asks.[3]

Nietzsche deals with eternal recurrence in more than one work. In *The Gay Science* Nietzsche renders his conception of eternal recur-rence and the dread he associates with it in this way:

What if some day or night a demon were to steal after you into your loneliest loneliness and say to you: 'This life as you now live it and have lived it, you will have to live once more and innu-merable times more; and there will be nothing new in it, but every pain and every joy and every thought and sigh and every-thing unutterably small or great in your life will have to return to you, all in the same succession and sequence.... The eternal hourglass of existence is turned upside down again and again and you with it, speck of dust.'

Would you not throw yourself down and gnash your teeth and curse the demon who spoke thus? Or have you once experienced a tremendous moment when you would have answered him: 'You are a god and never have I heard anything more divine.' If this thought gained possession of you, it would change you as you are or perhaps crush you. The question in each and every thing, 'Do you desire this once more and innumerable times more?' would lie upon your actions as the greatest weight. Or how well disposed would you have to become to yourself and to life *to crave nothing more fervently* than this ultimate eternal confirmation and seal?[4]

The idea of eternal recurrence is not original with Nietzsche. He had discovered it in his studies of the pre-Socratics, as Kaufmann points out, and the notion is set forth in a posthumously published book by Heine that Nietzsche had in his library.[5] Heine puts the idea as follows:

> For time is infinite, but the things in time, the concrete bodies, are finite. They may indeed disperse into the smallest particles; but these particles, the atoms, have their determinate number, and the number of configurations that, all of themselves, are formed out of them is also determinate. Now, however long a time may pass, according to the eternal laws governing the combinations of this eternal play of repetition, all configurations that have previously existed on this earth must yet meet, attract, repulse, kiss, and corrupt each other again....[6]

We need not concern ourselves with either the consistency or the truth of this doctrine. Our concern is with the role it plays in Zarathustra's trial of nausea. For Nietzsche there is something 'dreadful' in the very idea of an eternal recurrence. Yet, for Nietzsche, if one can muster the courage there is the possibility of fervent acceptance. Zarathustra in his triumph over nausea accepts the eternal recurrence of all that can happen or has happened, including the smallness of man. If all that can happen must happen, then the *Übermensch* will come – and this answers Zarathustra's question of the vision, 'Who is it who must yet come one day?' – but as the *Übermensch* will come and also eternally recur, so the small man will return and eternally recur. In his acceptance of eternal recurrence Zarathustra must accept, and does accept it, that the *Übermensch* cannot permanently displace the smallness of man.

For Nietzsche, in the passages from *Thus Spoke Zarathustra* and *The Gay Science* quoted above, what is particularly dreadful in eternal recurrence is the eternal recurrence of one's life as one has lived it and is now living it with all its pains and failures. For Zarathustra this is his life as he is living it in the midst of humankind's smallness. Allowing that eternal recurrence implies the recurrence of Zarathustra's actual life, we should note that

Nietzsche's concept of eternal recurrence also implies that every other possible life that Zarathustra might have led must also recur (what can occur must occur). Given eternal recurrence, Zarathustra just as he is, down to the last detail, will recur, but also he will recur with red hair and, in another return, he will recur as left-handed, and so on through an infinity of variations. But the fulcrum of Zarathustra's acceptance, for Nietzsche, is his embracing a return of the life he now has with all its failures and suffering before the smallness of humankind. In accepting his life and its eternal recurrence, Zarathustra accepts the eternal recurrence of the smallness of man.

Furthermore, when Zarathustra accepts eternal recurrence, he overcomes pity. As he tells the dwarf who is the spirit of gravity,

Courage is the best slayer: courage slays even pity....
   Courage... slays even death itself, for it says, 'Was *that* life? Well then! Once more!'[7]

Through the courage of his acceptance of eternal recurrence ('Was *that* life? Well then! Once more!') Zarathustra slays pity, for in his acceptance of eternal recurrence he accepts *all* of life and its eternal return. This is the connection between Zarathustra's two trials. So when Zarathustra accepts eternal recurrence he banishes pity. By overcoming nausea he overcomes pity (although at the point he addresses these words to the dwarf his trial of nausea before all that is small in human accomplishment is yet to come; and, in the Fourth Part, his banishment of pity will be tested in a trial of pity for the higher men).

When Zarathustra emerges from his seven-day trial, we are to understand, he has overcome nausea and accepted the eternal recurrence of his life, of all that has happened, and of the smallness of man. But how has he done this? All that we have seen so far is that he falls into a trance, as though he were dead, for seven days – and emerges triumphant over nausea with his acceptance of eternal recurrence. And how has he *joyfully* accepted eternal recurrence of all that has been – accepted it with the exuberant laughter of one transformed? This question, which is really our central question in this chapter, we shall take up shortly. First, though, let us connect Zarathustra's trial of nausea with what the author of *The Birth of Tragedy* identified as a similar trial of nausea for the 'Dionysian man'.

The Dionysian man, writes Nietzsche in *The Birth of Tragedy*.

> resembles Hamlet: both have once looked truly into the essence of things, they have *gained knowledge*, and nausea inhibits action; for their action could not change anything in the eternal nature of things.... [A]n insight into the horrible truth outweighs any motive for action, both in Hamlet and in the Dionysian man.
>
> ... Conscious of the truth he has once seen, man now sees everywhere only the horror or absurdity of existence; now he understands what is symbolic in Ophelia's fate; now he understands the wisdom of the sylvan god, Silenus: he is nauseated.[8]

The Dionysian man suffers nausea after glimpsing the underlying truth about things, the absurdity of existence. Now, Nietzsche says, he comes to understand the 'wisdom of ... Silenus'. Silenus is a god or demigod, a member of Dionysus' retinue, fat and old, a jovial reveller sometimes depicted with horse's ears, and always depicted as drinking or drunk. Silenus also was the tutor of Dionysus in his youth, and, though drunken, Silenus is full of wisdom. What is the wisdom of Silenus? It is, as found in antiquity and as Nietzsche repeats it, that it is best never to be born, but the second best is to die soon.[9] Traceable to Theognis in its earliest formulation, echoed by Sophocles in *Oedipus at Colonus*, this wisdom is debated by Hillel and Shammai in the first century of the Common Era and is found in the Book of Ecclesiastes (Eccl. 4:2–3).[10] Nietzsche may well have known it from Theognis, on whom he had written a thesis in Schulpforta before going to Bonn University, although the passage in *The Birth of Tragedy* closely follows an Aristotelian fragment from *Eudemus* or *On the Soul*. This Aristotelian fragment, in which Midas captures Silenus and induces him to deliver his wisdom, was quoted by Plutarch and Cicero.[11] And Nietzsche could have gleaned the reference from either source. Schopenhauer in *The World as Will and Representation*, where he tries to illustrate how widespread is the rejection of optimism, quotes Theognis, Sophocles, and many more up to Byron, all of whom echo the sentiment that it is better not to be born, or at least the sentiment that it is better to die than to live; however, Schopenhauer in this passage does not mention Silenus.[12] Nietzsche had read Schopenhauer long before he wrote *The Birth of Tragedy*. In short, Nietzsche could have encountered the wisdom of Silenus in any of several sources. In any case, for Nietzsche in *The Birth of Tragedy* it is Silenus' enervating wisdom that one comes to once one has gained insight into the way of things.

In both *The Birth of Tragedy* and *Thus Spoke Zarathustra*, then, there is an 'abysmal thought' or an 'insight' that once gained leads to nausea and the vitiation of action. In *The Birth of Tragedy* what nauseates the Dionysian man is the 'absurdity of existence', which leads to the wisdom of Silenus. In *Thus Spoke Zarathustra* it is the eternal recurrence of the smallness of man that nauseates Zarathustra – the smallness of his virtues and of his evil, the smallness that the madman of *The Gay Science* sees in the people in the market-place who cannot accept their deed, and that Zarathustra sees in even the higher men.

Now let us return to our concern with the character of Zarathustra's acceptance. Whence its joyfulness? For joyful it must be, reverberating with the happy laughter of one transformed it must be, in order for nausea to be overcome. This means that Zarathustra's acceptance must be very different from the soothsayer's acceptance. The soothsayer, who is encountered by Zarathustra more than once, is, like Zarathustra, an enunciator of wisdom. But he is in dialectical tension with Zarathustra. When the soothsayer first appears, in the Second Part, he proclaims, 'And I saw a great sadness descend upon mankind. The best grew weary of their works. A doctrine appeared, accompanied by a faith: "All is empty, all is the same, all has been".' 'Verily,' affirms the soothsayer, 'we have become too weary even to die.'[13] We should notice that the burden of what the soothsayer proclaims, and accepts, is not that different from the absurdity of existence – 'all is empty' – and also echoes the idea of an eternal recurrence – 'all is the same, all has been'. The dialectical tension between the soothsayer and Zarathustra arises from the contrast between their modes of acceptance.

The soothsayer accepts the hard truth of the emptiness of existence, but his acceptance is the acceptance of weariness. For Zarathustra, weariness gives up on the world; it is weariness, he says (in a passage that we quoted in Chapter 5), that creates all gods and afterworlds and that 'does not want to want any more'. In *Twilight of the Idols* Nietzsche says the following about the 'consensus of the sages' and 'weariness of life'. 'Concerning life', Nietzsche says,

the wisest men of all ages have judged alike: *it is no good.* Always
and everywhere one has heard the same sound from their
mouths – a sound full of doubt, full of melancholy, full of weariness of life, full of resistance to life.

Nietzsche goes on to mention Socrates and to allude to
Schopenhauer; however, he could hardly have addressed the soothsayer more directly. And he says: 'At least something must be *sick*
here'.[14] Nietzsche does not argue against the truth of the soothsayer's doctrine, just as he does not argue against the truth of the
wisdom of Silenus. What he objects to is the 'sound' that comes out
of the mouths of sages like the soothsayer: what is sick is the weariness they evince, not the hard truth of their enunciations.

The soothsayer's weary acceptance of the emptiness and same-
ness of life is the antithesis of Zarathustra's joyful acceptance of the
eternal recurrence of all life and existence. The soothsayer's weariness is very like infinite resignation. In infinite resignation, we will
recall, one still wants what one gives up, though one, we may say,
has stopped wanting to want it or wants to stop wanting it. One is
resigned to the loss of what one has given up, and in this sense
accepts one's loss, but there is no joyfulness in that acceptance.
Zarathustra's acceptance, by way of contrast, is – must be – joyful.
This is so even though 'the proverb of Zarathustra' is 'What does it
matter?' Zarathustra pronounces this proverb twice toward the end
of *Thus Spoke Zarathustra*, once at the very end, when he finally and
completely renounces his pity for the higher men and for suffering:
What does it matter?[15] Zarathustra's proverb sounds like an expression of infinite resignation or an attitude very close to it, but, at the
same time, it is intended to be very different from an expression of
the soothsayer's weariness. Even if the burden of Zarathustra's
proverb is similar to the burden of the soothsayer's enunciation of
emptiness, nevertheless the affective response that Zarathustra's
proverb expresses must not be weariness or sadness or the repose
of infinite resignation. It must be an expression of his joyful acceptance – or at least not negate it.

'Joy', proclaims Zarathustra in the Fourth Part, 'wants itself,
wants eternity, wants recurrence, wants everything eternally the
same'.[16] And in the Third Part, close after his trial of nausea,
Zarathustra looks into the eyes of life, dances with life, weeps with
life, and proclaims 'life was dearer to me than all my wisdom ever
was': and, as the heavy bell sounds the hours, 'Joy – deeper yet

than agony' and 'But all joy wants eternity'.[17] Immediately there follows the section entitled 'The Seven Seals' – Zarathustra's revelatory seven seals – each with the same refrain, ending with: '*For I love you, O eternity*'.[18] Here, unmistakably, is the joyfulness of Zarathustra's acceptance of eternal recurrence. So Zarathustra joyfully accepts eternity. But that was really never in question. Our question is: How is it that Zarathustra's acceptance is joyful? Whence his joy? Perhaps Nietzsche would agree with Camus in *The Myth of Sisyphus* that happiness and the absurd are 'two sons of the same earth'.[19] But this does not take us very far. Whence Zarathustra's joy in accepting either the absurdity of all that is or the eternal recurrence of all that exists, especially all that is small? Its source, it seems, is in the *means* of Zarathustra's acceptance.

The means of Zarathustra's acceptance is, at bottom, his will, his wilful doing. Let us return to Zarathustra's vision: by an effort of will the shepherd bites off the head of the snake (just as Sisyphus by his will rolls the stone up his mountain – Sisyphus, whom Camus says we must imagine happy).[20] However, there is more to Zarathustra's effort, to his wilful endeavour. Through his simply willing to do so, we can allow, Zarathustra succeeds in *accepting* eternal recurrence – symbolized by the shepherd's screwing up his courage and biting off the head of the snake. But there is more to what he wills, and it is this further wilful exercise that accounts for the *joyfulness* in Zarathustra's acceptance.

It is at this point that we should direct our attention to several related sections (or chapters) in *Thus Spoke Zarathustra*. It is not quite accurate to describe these sections as Zarathustra's speeches. In them Zarathustra is not proclaiming any part of his message. Each is closer to poetry, turning on imagery and metaphor; and in each when Zarathustra speaks, or sings, his words are a lyrical evocation. Together these sections form a pattern that tells us much about the means of Zarathustra's joyful acceptance.

The first of these sections, coming in the Second Part of *Thus Spoke Zarathustra*, is 'The Dancing Song'. Zarathustra discovers girls dancing upon a green meadow. When they see Zarathustra they stop, but Zarathustra entreats them to continue. Cupid is asleep nearby. Zarathustra tells the girls that he will sing a song as they and Cupid dance. The song that Zarathustra composes on the spot and sings begins by addressing life, personified as a woman, and continues by recounting an exchange he has had with her. 'Into your eyes I looked recently, O life!', Zarathustra's song begins. 'And into the unfathomable I then seemed to be sinking. But you pulled me out with a golden fishing rod. ...' When Zarathustra calls life unfathomable she replies that she is merely changeable and accuses him and men of presenting her with men's virtues. As the song continues, Zarathustra brings in another female figure, his own wisdom. The only reason he praises life, she angrily tells Zarathustra, is that '[y]ou will, you want, you love'. In Zarathustra's song the three of them – life, Zarathustra and his wisdom – form a kind of lovers' triangle. Zarathustra says: 'I love only life – and verily, most of all when I hate life.' And Zarathustra says that he is so well disposed toward wisdom, his wisdom, 'because she reminds me so much of life'. 'Who is this wisdom?', life once asked him, Zarathustra's song runs. And Zarathustra answered that one thirsts after her and is never satisfied – perhaps 'she is evil and false and a female in every way'. At this, life laughs sarcastically and asks if Zarathustra is speaking of her. The song ends with Zarathustra addressing life: 'Ah, and then you opened your eyes again, O beloved life. And again I seemed to myself to be sinking into the unfathomable'. The dance ends, the girls who were dancing on the meadow depart. Zarathustra grows sad and reflects, 'Is it not folly still to be alive?'[21]

This section comes in *Thus Spoke Zarathustra* well before Zarathustra's vision of the shepherd and his subsequent trial of nausea, and in this section there is no hint of joyful acceptance. Yet this dancing song prefigures what is to come. We find in it an ambivalence on Zarathustra's part toward life: he loves life and at the same time he hates life. We find in it Zarathustra's sense of the tension between his wisdom and life, along with his sense of their closeness, as indicated by the feminine symbol for both and by life herself taking his comments about wisdom to apply to her. We find, anticipating Zarathustra's nausea, his sense that he is sinking into the unfathomable depths of life. And, most significantly perhaps for our concern, we find that the dancing sustains Zarathustra, so that when it comes to an end he is overtaken by sadness, a sadness deep enough to make being alive seem to be folly, quite in accord with the wisdom of Silenus.

The next section to be noted is entitled 'The Other Dancing Song'. It comes in the Third Part, after Zarathustra's vision and trial, and at once echoes the first dancing song and more clearly speaks to Zarathustra's trial of nausea. 'Into your eyes I looked recently, O life', begins this section, and it continues, 'I saw gold blinking in your night-eye; my heart stopped in delight....' Zarathustra is 'frantic to dance' and leaps after life, who flees back, her hair sweeping against Zarathustra. She turns, her eyes 'full of desire'. Zarathustra dances after her. Her evil eyes flash as they dance. She is a 'malicious leaping belle'. As Zarathustra leaps he falls. Zarathustra would carry life to a place where shepherds are playing their flutes. But she apparently slips away, and Zarathustra exclaims, 'Oh, this damned nimble, supple snake and slippery witch!' And the first part of 'The Other Dancing Song' ends with: 'You witch, if I have so far sung to you, now you shall cry. ... Or have I forgotten the whip? Not I!'[22]

Then life answers Zarathustra. She entreats Zarathustra not to crack his whip, for 'noise murders thought'. And she says to Zarathustra that they are 'both two real good-for-nothings and evil-for-nothings'. 'Beyond good and evil we found our island and our green meadow....' ('Evil' for the author of *The Antichrist* and *Beyond Good and Evil*, we should keep in mind, is the term that the religious and the weak use to designate what is strong and life-affirming.) She confesses that she is jealous of Zarathustra's wisdom and says to him: 'If your wisdom ever ran away from you, then my love would quickly run away too.' To this she adds softly: 'O Zarathustra, you are not faithful enough to me. You do not love me nearly as much as you say; I know that you are thinking of leaving me soon.' Then life and Zarathustra look at each other and weep together. And Zarathustra confesses that then 'life was dearer to me than all my wisdom ever was'. There follow the twelve strokes of the hour-tolling bell, ending with:

Ten!

'But all joy wants eternity –

Eleven!

'Wants deep, wants deep eternity.'

Twelve![23]

The next section is entitled 'The Seven Seals'. Each of its seven parts ends with:

Oh, how should I not lust after eternity [nach der Ewigkeit brünstig sein] and after the nuptial ring of rings, the ring of recurrence?

Never yet have I found the woman from whom I wanted children, unless it be this woman whom I love: for I love you, O
eternity.

For I love you, O eternity![24]

Earlier I quoted the very end of this refrain, as I quoted from 'The
Other Dancing Song', in order to establish that as Nietzsche presents Zarathustra's acceptance of eternal recurrence it is joyful.

It is not accidental that 'The Seven Seals' follows 'The Other
Dancing Song'. Zarathustra's passion for life has been transferred to
eternity, and both are symbolized by a female figure. And the joyfulness of his acceptance of eternal recurrence takes the form of his
ardour for the female figure of eternity. What is important here,
given our concern with the source of Zarathustra's joyfulness, is not
the personification of life or of eternity; nor is it Zarathustra's acceptance being expressed as his passionate love for a female figure that
symbolizes eternity. At least these elements in and of themselves are
not what is important. What we should note is the metaphorical role
of these female figures in their interaction with Zarathustra.

In the first dancing-song Zarathustra does not enter into the
dance himself. He sings a song to life as girls dance upon the
meadow. In the second dancing-song Zarathustra does enter
the dance: he and life dance together. And they are not dancing a
minuet. Her hair whips against Zarathustra; the two partners leap
about in their dance. The girls who dance with each other in the
first dancing-song are not presented as whirling or leaping. We
might picture them as the three dancing Graces in Botticelli's *La
Primavera* – Botticelli's three Graces delicately holding hands as
they move in a gentle circle. Nothing in Nietzsche's description of
the dancing girls on the meadow contradicts this picture. As I have
noted, 'The Dancing Song' prefigures what is to come, including
'The Other Dancing Song'. However, what is lacking in the first
dancing-song is Zarathustra's joyfulness. On the other hand, it is
explicit in 'The Other Dancing Song'. The difference between the
two is that, in the second, Zarathustra himself dances, and he
dances a frenetic dance not devoid of sexual overtones. In fact it is
not devoid of suggestions of violence. The image of the dance in
'The Other Dancing Song' is, in short, Dionysian. The source of
Zarathustra's joy is akin to the source of ecstasy in the rites of
Dionysus, which of course were familiar to the author of *The Birth
of Tragedy*.

When, in the second part of 'The Other Dancing Song', life answers Zarathustra and rebukes him for cracking his whip, the level of energy lessens. The dancing stops and life speaks calmly to Zarathustra, but what she tells him is emotionally charged: she knows, she says, that he is thinking of leaving her soon. Zarathustra does not deny this, but whispers something into her ear. The text is silent about what Zarathustra whispers, although life is surprised that Zarathustra knows such a thing. (Kaufmann suggests that what Zarathustra whispers is that after his death he will recur eternally.)[25] At this point they weep together. The dancing has stopped, but the high state of emotion that it generated is still in force. In the last part of 'The Other Dancing Song', the part with the twelve strokes of the bell, Nietzsche makes for the first time an explicit connection between joy and eternal recurrence. This connection carries over into the next section, 'The Seven Seals', in which, as we have noted, Zarathustra affirms his joyful acceptance of eternal recurrence through proclaiming his love, his ardour, for the female figure of eternity, who seemingly replaces the female figure of life in Zarathustra's affections. To be noted here are two connections: the first connection is that between the two female figures or symbols, eternity and life, which is such that the second, as it were, emerges from the first. This, I believe, is in accord with Nietzsche's thinking; in order fully to accept life one must accept eternal recurrence. The second connection to be noted is that between Zarathustra's active entry into the dance and his joyful acceptance of life/eternity. In the first dancing-song Zarathustra is ambivalent toward life – he loves and hates her – and she is confused with that other female figure, Zarathustra's wisdom. In 'The Other Dancing Song' Zarathustra enters the dance and he would passionately love life, who, Zarathustra says, is dearer to him than his wisdom, from whom she clearly stands apart. If we put these two connections together we can see that the source of Zarathustra's *joyful* acceptance of eternal recurrence is, or is continuous with, his joyful acceptance of life, and we can see that its source is something he does, something symbolized by the metaphor of his entering into a frenetic dance that engenders Dionysian emotions.

The last section in the pattern of sections before us occurs in the Fourth Part of *Thus Spoke Zarathustra*, quite near the end of the work: it is 'The Drunken Song'. In 'The Drunken Song' also there is dancing, although in this instance it is the dancing of the higher men, who have gathered at Zarathustra's cave. They, as we noted in Chapter 6, revert to religious belief, to 'religious' belief in an ass. But in another turn, which occurs in 'The Drunken Song', they renounce their reversion to religious worship. The ugliest man announces: 'For the sake of this day, I am for the first time satisfied that I have lived my whole life.... Living on earth is worth while: one day, one festival with Zarathustra taught me to love the earth'. In this way he renounces his reversion. The ugliest man continues in his exuberance: '"Was *that* life?" I want to say to death. "Well then! Once more!"' So it is that the ugliest man affirms life and the return of his life – using the very words that Zarathustra had used earlier in addressing the dwarf. The ugliest man then invites the other higher men to join him in their own affirmation of life, which they do.[26]

And the higher men begin to dance with joy, some laughing, some crying. Even the soothsayer renounces weariness. And, we are told, there are some who relate that the ass danced too. Is Zarathustra jubilant? No, he is not. And we are given, in its first statement, 'the proverb of Zarathustra', which says: 'What does it matter?' In the text the proverb could be read as: What does it matter whether the ass danced or not? But the more profound sense of it is: What does it matter that the higher men have made a significant move toward the *Übermensch*? One might think it matters a lot – for Zarathustra and for Nietzsche. But Zarathustra's acceptance of eternal recurrence – his joyful acceptance of eternal recurrence – is such that neither the smallness nor the greatness of human achievement matters.

Zarathustra stands before the higher men 'like a drunkard'. His eyes grow dim. His drunkenness is not that of the vine, but that of the spirit as it embraces life with all its agony and pain in a Dionysian embrace. Zarathustra begins to speak with the inspiration of his intoxification, and in what follows he whispers the meaning of what was told to him by the hour-striking bell in 'The Other Dancing Song'.[27] He elaborates each aphorism that accompanied a bell-stroke, including that which accompanied the last bell-stroke at the very end of 'The Other Dancing Song', quoted above – 'Wants deep, wants deep eternity'. Zarathustra proclaims:

> All eternal joy wants itself, hence it also wants agony. O happiness, O pain! Oh, break, heart! You higher men, do learn this, joy wants eternity. Joy wants the eternity of *all* things, *wants deep, wants deep eternity*.[28]

Zarathustra does not dance with the higher men but, as he lyrically elaborates the meaning of what the bell said, his 'soul dances'.[29] However, the distinctive element of 'The Drunken Song' is the drunkenness, or inspiration, of Zarathustra's spirit, which is itself Dionysian. Drunkenness as such, we may say, is Dionysian. But Zarathustra's drunkenness is not that of alcoholic revelry, it is that of the spirit; and it has its sources in Zarathustra's will. Nietzsche is very far from suggesting that Zarathustra has *received* inspiration. His inspiration is in his drunkenness, and his drunkenness he has brought upon himself by his own exercise of will.

Zarathustra not only dances, he sings. In the first dancing-song, he composes and sings a song. But the second dancing-song, 'The Other Dancing Song', is also a song, as is the 'The Drunken Song'. Zarathustra in 'The Drunken Song' is not analytically explicating the aphorisms of the bell-strokes; he is poetically elaborating them – he is singing. The source of his joyful drunkenness is what he does, what he wills to do, his poetic singing. It is not something he has reasoned out. Nor is the source of his joyful drunkenness an insight into anything; certainly it is not an insight into the goodness of life. It has nothing to do with anything he has discovered. His doing, his poetic singing, induces his drunkenness, but it is not that his drunkenness causes his joy. Zarathustra's drunkenness *is* his joy. It is not the cause of his joy in the way that alcoholic drunkenness might cause one to be gleeful.

Nietzsche is well aware of the power of the dance and of song to bring about a profound change in our emotions. In *The Birth of Tragedy* Nietzsche says this:

> when the danger to his will [the will of one who is nauseated by the horrible truth about existence] is greatest *art* approaches as a saving sorceress, expert at healing. She alone knows how to turn these thoughts about the horror or absurdity of existence into notions with which one can live.... The satyr chorus of the dithyramb is the saving deed of Greek art; faced with the intermediary world of these Dionysian companions, the feelings described here [horror and absurdity] exhausted themselves.[30]

In *The Birth of Tragedy* Nietzsche allows that art – dithyrambic song and dance – can bring about acceptance of the horror and absurdity of life. In *Thus Spoke Zarathustra* it is life/eternity that is accepted, and one's entering the dance and one's singing – not one's hearing the satyr chorus – that are 'the saving deed'. But the underlying perception of the power of the Dionysian is the same.[31]

For Nietzsche the joyfulness of acceptance is precipitated by Dionysian means, and the means of attaining joy influences the character of the joy attained. It is a Dionysian joyfulness symbolized by the frenetic ecstasy of the dance and drunkenness. Joy is deeper than agony, Zarathustra says or sings in 'The Drunken Song', but also joy *wants* agony. Joy as the breathless ecstasy of the dance, and the joyfulness of intoxication, embraces agony, in the sense that Dionysian ecstasy is continuous with and emerges from the physical exhaustion of frenetic dancing or from the intoxication of drunkenness. Zarathustra's joy wants agony, not just in the sense that agony is a part of the all that Zarathustra joyfully accepts, but in the sense that his joy includes the experience of agony.

To summarize: at bottom, in Nietzsche's presentation, Zarathustra's joyful acceptance of life and of eternity – of life/eternity – is something he does or brings about through his wilful endeavour. For Nietzsche the acceptance of life/eternity is an act of will, a courageous act of will, symbolized by the shepherd's biting off the head of the black snake of nausea. But, moreover, as I have tried to bring out, for Nietzsche in *Thus Spoke Zarathustra* the *joyful* acceptance of life/eternity is a matter of wilful endeavour. It is something that Zarathustra brings about through his own will, by his entering the dance with life, or rather, what Zarathustra's entering the dance metaphorically represents, and by his lyrical singing, his poetic expression of, his affirmation of, life/eternity. What do Zarathustra's dancing and singing represent? Zarathustra's dancing does not represent physical dancing (any more than Johannes de Silentio's likening of the knight of faith's movement of infinity to the movement of a ballet dancer indicates a physical movement on the part of the knight of faith). In 'The Drunken Song' Zarathustra's *soul* dances. What of Zarathustra's singing? Whenever Zarathustra sings, Nietzsche sings. When Zarathustra sings in the dancing and drunken songs, Nietzsche has Zarathustra lyrically and poetically express, and also thereby *create*, his – their – joyfulness. Zarathustra creates his joyfulness through the resolution of his will, and it is for this reason that Nietzsche can urge others to follow him with their own joyful acceptance through a like exercise of their own wills.

Part III

9

The Joy of Faith and the Joy of Zarathustra's Acceptance

We come now to the central question of our study: How does the joy of faith compare to the joy of Zarathustra's acceptance? Our question, of course, relates to the joy of faith as faith is presented in *Fear and Trembling*, and it relates to Zarathustra's acceptance of life, and its eternal recurrence, as his acceptance is presented in *Thus Spoke Zarathustra*. More nicely expressed, our question is: How does the joy of the knight of faith compare to the joy of Zarathustra's acceptance of life/eternity?

It is not accidental that both Kierkegaard and Nietzsche give great importance to joy. Each in his own way is addressing the old question, What is a fulfilled human life? At bottom each is giving us a picture of life lived most meaningfully. Of course their pictures are very different. However, each senses, I think, that it would be odd, even deeply counterintuitive, if a fulfilled life should *not* be a life joyfully accepted.

Kierkegaard, or Johannes de Silentio, and Nietzsche are clear, even emphatic, that their respective heroes, the knight of faith and Zarathustra, are joyful. For Johannes de Silentio faith by its nature is joyful, and for Nietzsche the full acceptance of life/eternity is joyful. Their concurrence about the necessity of joy in their respective heroes does not mean that what is joy for the one is joy for the other. However, though the joy of the one may not be the joy of the other, nevertheless, we should concede, the joy of each is indeed joy. Neither the joy of Abraham nor the joy of Zarathustra is merely the absence of sadness or acceptance without complaint or habitual and unreflective acceptance. Neither the joy of the one nor the joy of the other is the response of infinite resignation, nor is either mere contentment, perhaps induced in oneself by dulling one's mind (as by 'chewing the cud').

There are two cardinal differences between the joy of the knight of faith and the joy of Zarathustra. The first difference has to do

107

with the difference between passion and emotion. For Kierkegaard and Johannes de Silentio, faith is a passion. As such, for Kierkegaard, it is not a feeling or emotion but a state of the whole person. (Feelings are immediate and so, for Kierkegaard, in the sphere of the 'aesthetic'.)[1] Kierkegaard would agree with Nietzsche, as we noted in Chapter 5, that 'the kingdom of heaven' is a state of the heart. In *The Antichrist* Nietzsche goes on to say that Christianity is '[n]ot a faith' but a 'state of being'.[2] For Kierkegaard, and for Johannes, faith is not opposed to a state of being; it *is* a state of being (although not a state of being once and for all achieved). As a passion it is a state of being of the whole person. It does not follow from faith's being a passion that the joy of faith is also a passion, but so I think Johannes would understand it. If it is a passion, it is not a feeling (even if it should involve having certain feelings). Another passion Johannes compares to faith is love, the romantic love between a man and a woman. In each case one has one's 'whole life' in it.[3] In *Fear and Trembling* the joy of faith is not a momentary feeling of elation, it is the affective dimension of the state of faith. Abraham's joy is a part of his state of being, his faith, not an episode that punctuates his faith. In this respect, though in no other, the joy of faith is like the response of infinite resignation.

We can see in another way that the joy of faith for knights of faith is a state of their being and not an episodic feeling. The joy that pervades Abraham flows from his certitude that Isaac will not be lost to him; and the joy of other knights of faith, who have the faith of Abraham, flows from their certitude that all will be well. ('All will be well' is the Bible-echoing phrase that, I suggested in Chapter 4, expresses the direct object of the faith of a contemporary knight of faith; of course, it also covers Abraham's more specific belief that Isaac will not be lost to him.) Abraham's certitude or knowledge that Isaac will not be lost to him, and the certitude or knowledge of other knights of faith that all will be well, is a mental state, or better, a state of their being, which expresses itself in the confidence of their action and in the joy of their faith. As their certitude or knowledge is a state and not an episode of consciousness, so the joy that comes of their certitude or knowledge and accompanies their faith is not an episode.

By contrast, the joy of Zarathustra's acceptance *is* an episode – a feeling of delight or elation, a feeling of intense, even ecstatic pleasure – induced by the means symbolized by dance and poetic singing wilfully taken up. Zarathustra's joy is like the Dionysian feelings precipitated by the Dionysian rites that Zarathustra's dancing resembles. It is a kind of ecstasy. Ida Overbeck, the wife of Nietzsche's close friend Franz Overbeck, in her recollections of Nietzsche, suggests that Nietzsche in his own efforts to overcome disgust, or nausea – that which he expresses in 'The Convalescent' in the Third Part of *Zarathustra* – 'resort[ed] ... to mystical artistic ecstasy'.[4]

In 'The Other Dancing Song' the German word that is translated as 'joy' is *Lust*. So too later in 'The Drunken Song'. *Lust* can be translated as joy or delight and also as lust or carnal desire. In its connotative range *Lust* is different from *Freude*, the German word that Nietzsche uses when he criticizes the voluntary beggar for denying the 'joys of the flesh' [*fleischlichen Freuden*].[5] Given the imagery of Zarathustra's dance with life in 'The Other Dancing Song', given its sexual and even violent overtones, it may well be that Nietzsche wanted the sexual suggestion of *Lust*. However, whatever sexual penumbra it may have, Zarathustra's joy is an emotional feeling that comes upon him. It is not a state, like being happy. It is certainly not the contentment, the 'happiness on earth [*Das Glück auf Erden*]' urged by the voluntary beggar and embodied in his cows.[6] Neither, however, is it happiness in a more human sense, or in any sense. 'Am I concerned with *happiness* [*Glück*]?' Zarathustra rhetorically asks at the end of *Thus Spoke Zarathustra*. No, he is not. 'I am concerned with my *work*', he proclaims.[7] Zarathustra's final acceptance of life/eternity is a joyful acceptance, and Zarathustra's joy is his feeling of delight, of elation, which takes its character from the means by which it comes upon him.

And this brings us to the second difference between the joy of faith in *Fear and Trembling* and Zarathustra's joyful acceptance. They are utterly different in their provenance. The source of Zarathustra's joy is the means by which he precipitates his joy. These means are symbolized by the metaphor of the dance, Dionysian dance, and by the metaphor of Zarathustra's drunken singing in the drunkenness of his soul. What Zarathustra brings about in himself, we should keep in mind, is a joyful *acceptance*, a joyful acceptance of life and of eternity. He would have no sympathy for the sort of suggestion made by Aldous Huxley that 'our suffering species' needs a 'new drug' to allow it periodically to escape from the monotony of life.[8] For

Nietzsche life as it is, with its pains and even its monotony, is to be embraced joyfully, not escaped from. If this cannot be done, eternal recurrence of life with all its smallness cannot be joyfully accepted.

The essential point regarding the provenance of Zarathustra's joy is that which we saw in the last chapter: Zarathustra's joyful acceptance is a product of his will, an effort that is symbolized by his entering a Dionysian dance and becoming drunk with a drunkenness of the soul. The provenance of the joy of the knight of faith is not his or her own will. It is the knight's confident awareness of God's goodness, expressed in trust in God and trust that all manner of thing will be well. The trust of knights of faith is absolute and their faith is certain. They *know* that all manner of thing will be well. That is, given that knights of faith are as they understand themselves to be, they know that in the light of God's goodness all manner of thing will be well: thus their certainty and lack of doubt. The provenance of their joy is what has been given to them to know with full certainty about the goodness of God's way. The provenance of the joy of knights of faith is not a wilful doing, not a precipitating act of will; it is this *knowledge* that has been given to them. How different from Zarathustra! Zarathustra's joy is *in spite of* what he is certain of or firmly believes. As Zarathustra is presented in *Thus Spoke Zarathustra*, his joy is in spite of what he *knows*. What he knows is his 'abysmal thought': he knows that all that is small will eternally recur. His joy is not grounded in this knowledge. His joy in accepting this thought must come in spite of his knowledge of its truth; thus the necessity of his Dionysian means of overcoming this nauseating truth.

To be sure, there is for Abraham in his trial of faith, in Johannes' retelling, a role for will and the exertion of will. But Abraham's joy does not come to him through what he wills or accomplishes by his wilful endeavour. Granted – and for Johannes this is to be insisted upon – Abraham must exert his will to carry out God's command. Though he knows Isaac will live, he must bend his will to overcome his anxiety, to take Isaac to Moriah and to raise the knife. And Abraham, like the knights of faith that may follow him, must through his will make the double movement of infinity continuously. In making the double movement the knights must resign all infinitely and then grasp it again through the absurd – although Johannes de Silentio is clear that one's own strength, while sufficient for the first movement, is not sufficient for the movement that brings one to faith.[9]

However, in any case, Abraham's joy, which attends his faith and is part of its passion, is not precipitated by Abraham's will, by something he does that might be symbolized by his dancing. This is so even though Johannes uses the image of the leap for the movement of faith. The knight of faith is like a ballet dancer, Johannes allows at one point, yet the knight makes the movements of infinity so apparently effortlessly that nothing in his appearance betrays anything other than the pedestrian.[10] It is interesting that both Nietzsche and Kierkegaard use as metaphors the dance, although for the one it is the exuberant dance of Dionysian frenzy and for the other the invisible movement of a perfect ballet leap. They both use this metaphor because, for Nietzsche, the life of Zarathustra involves a doing, a striving, and, for Kierkegaard in *Fear and Trembling*, the life of faith does as well. But this is not to say that the two authors locate wilful striving at the same point in the lives of their respective heroes, and in fact they do not. There is nothing in Johannes' portrait of Abraham that corresponds to the shepherd's biting off the head of the snake that was lodged in his throat. Although Abraham must carry out God's command in anxiety, he nevertheless receives it and acts upon it with trust in God's goodness and absolute confidence that all will be well. In the same way, Abraham need not precipitate in himself the affective side of his acceptance. He is joyful because he knows God will not take Isaac from him.

As faith is presented in *Fear and Trembling*, the source of the joy of the knights of faith is their knowledge of God's goodness. But what is the source of this knowledge? In the case of Abraham – Kierkegaard's paradigmatic knight of faith in *Fear and Trembling* – what he knows is specifically that God in His goodness will not take Isaac from him. How does Abraham know that Isaac will not be taken from him? Within the story of Abraham as Johannes presents it, Abraham knows because God has given him His promise. The answer to the *internal* question 'How does Abraham know?' is 'He knows because God has given His promise.' God's promise to Abraham that through Isaac he will be the father of nations is barely mentioned by Johannes.[11] Yet, as I see it, in Johannes' exploration of Abraham's trial it towers in the background above Mount Moriah, for it is absolutely essential for the *Fear and Trembling* portrait of Abraham's faith. In Genesis 17 God speaks to Abraham and gives him His promise. Abraham's experience in Genesis is an experience of the living God, an experience of God in fear and trembling in which Abraham falls upon the ground before God (Gen. 17:3). Abraham not only receives God's promise but receives it in such a way that he is certain of its divine origin. Abraham's experience of God, however, is left in the background by Kierkegaard and the pseudonymous Johannes. But this experience is internally necessary to the story, especially in Kierkegaard's construction, for it is within his experience of God that Abraham receives God's specific promise that through Isaac he, Abraham, will be the father of nations. Only in the light of this promise, and his abiding sense that it is from God, does Abraham know – can he have no doubt and have the certainty of faith – that Isaac will live.

Also necessary to Kierkegaard's construction is Abraham's knowing that it is God who commands him to take Isaac to Moriah. Kierkegaard does not raise the question of how he knows it is God who speaks and not Satan or a delusion. Sartre does, as we have noted (in Chapter 2), and such a question may be asked. At the same time we should note that in Kierkegaard's construction it is a given within the story of Abraham that Abraham knows. In a way it can be an embarrassment for Kierkegaard's construction of the trial of Abraham that the reader is given no answer to Sartre's question. However, as far as contemporary knights of faith are concerned, there is no issue here. This is because, in accord with what we observed in Chapter 4, they have not received God's promise that they will be given a son, nor have they been commanded to sacrifice their sons. Neither have they been promised any finite thing in this world. Contemporary knights of faith, if there are any, do not have God's promise that their sons will live, or that they will have health or wealth or anything else in this domain, and they do not have, let us allow, a direct experience of God's speaking to them in the language of their daily commerce. They do not believe, as a direct object of their faith, that they will be given or not lose this or that particular finite thing. Yet, as I argued (in Chapter 4) and have been assuming, we should allow that their faith does have a non-specific direct object, which, like the direct object of Abraham's faith, is propositional and is logically tied to trust in God. Contemporary knights of faith must believe with certainty and see themselves as knowing that God's goodness is present in their lives, that – in the formulation I have been using – all will be well. This they believe, and, if they are as they see themselves, this they know to be true. And so we find that we can ask: How do contemporary knights of faith know that all will be well?

The answer cannot be the kind of direct experience of God that Abraham is depicted as having in Genesis. Contemporary knights have not spoken to God face to face and received His promise of any finite thing in this world. But their knowledge of God's goodness, and so that all will be well, could still be grounded in an analogue of Abraham's experience of God. As I suggested in Chapter 4, contemporary knights may come to knowledge of God's goodness through an experience like the Psalmist's experience of the living God. In his experience the Psalmist comes into the presence of God when he lifts up his eyes to the hills and in the daily events of his life. The Psalmist discovers God's goodness through experiencing, in fear and trembling, God's goodness in His living presence in the world. And with this experience comes a deepened trust in God and an abiding sense that all will be well:

> thou anointest my head with oil, my cup overflows.
> Surely goodness and mercy shall follow me all the days of my life (Ps. 23:5–6).

If we allow that, within the world of the Psalms, this experience was available to the Psalmist, we can allow that it is available to knights of faith who are in the Psalmist's tradition. Accordingly, we should allow that this discovery-experience can be the source of contemporary knights' knowledge that all will be well. That is, we should allow that this kind of discovery-experience is countenanced as a possible source of religious knowledge within the religious heritage in which knights of faith stand.[12]

It is to be noted that knights of faith coming to know through such a discovery-experience is in a finer way in accord with *Fear and Trembling*. Johannes tells us that Abraham and other knights of faith believe and act by virtue of the absurd – by virtue of what is beyond 'human calculation', as Johannes puts it. And, in the same way (although Johannes does not explicitly say so), if knights of faith know, they come to know by virtue of the absurd. To say that they come to know by virtue of the absurd is to say that they come to know in a way that is not countenanced by what is generally understood or accepted – they come to know by what is beyond 'human calculation'. This of course would be just the case if knights come to know by virtue of the Psalmist's experience of God's presence.

I am not arguing that the Psalmist's mode of discovery is the only means countenanced by the traditions of Christianity by which a knight of faith could come to knowledge of God's good-ness. There are others that might be put forward, ranging from the disclosure of the Bible to the witnessing of a miracle. I am arguing that such a discovery-experience is *an* analogue of Abraham's ex-perience, that it is an *experiential* analogue, and that, as an analogue of Abraham's experience, it could, without violating the religious tradition in which knights of faith stand, provide the religious knowledge needed by the *Fear and Trembling* model of faith.

In short, the kind of discovery-experience we find implicit in the Psalms and in other religious settings would fill the cognitive gap in the picture of contemporary knights of faith we obtain when we extend the *Fear and Trembling* conception of faith. And this is so even though Johannes does not explore this question or contem-plate the sorts of religious experience that knights of faith might have. In fact Kierkegaard is suspicious of religious experience, es-pecially 'direct' experience, for it would seem to belong to the 'im-mediate'. Yet, as we noted in Chapter 4, in *Fear and Trembling* for Kierkegaard, or for Johannes de Silentio, faith is 'a later immedia-cy', and in the *Postscript* Kierkegaard, or Johannes Climacus, allows that after one has entered a God-relationship one can see God everywhere.

At issue between Kierkegaard and Nietzsche is the possibility of such a discovery-experience. If the model of faith in *Fear and Trembling* is fully embodied in the lives of living individuals, then those individuals must have knowledge of God's goodness. In some way they must come to know that through God's goodness all will be well. Presupposed by Kierkegaard and Johannes in their *Fear and Trembling* account of Abraham's trial of faith is Abraham's receiving God's promise, through which he knows that all will be well and Isaac will not be lost to him. That is, it is presupposed *in-ternally*; if we say, furthermore, that there really was an Abraham who really did know that Isaac would live, then it is presupposed *externally*. By extension, the *Fear and Trembling* postulation of con-temporary knights of faith presupposes *some* analogue of Abraham's experience through which they come to know that all will be well. Such an analogue is presupposed *internally* as a part of the self-understanding of contemporary knights of faith, and it is presupposed *externally* if we allow that there are now or ever have been in existence knights of faith who fully embody the model of faith in *Fear and Trembling*. One such – and, in fact, a pre-eminent – analogue would be a discovery-experience, like the Psalmist's experience, of God and His goodness with its resultant trust in God and its joyful knowledge that all is well. It is presupposed by Nietzsche, on the other hand, that Abraham had no experience of God, that there is no analogue of Abraham's experience available to anyone, and that, specifically, the discovery-experience of the Psalmist is available to no one. For Nietzsche there is no such experience since there is no God. God is dead and has never existed; all belief in God has its source in a weariness of life, not in an experience of God.[13]

At the root of the matter two very different intuitions divide Kierkegaard and Nietzsche. For Nietzsche, will is at the centre of our human existence. Morality is importantly a matter of individual creation, that is, of will. We must will to be bridges to the *Übermensch*. The very basis of life is will to power. So it is not surprising that, for Nietzsche, the joyfulness of the acceptance of life and eternity is a product of our willing. Nietzsche wants to show us the path to joyful acceptance of a Godless universe – a joyful acceptance that is as much a matter of our own creation as the morality we live.

Across this intuitional chasm stands Kierkegaard. For Kierkegaard faith, or faith on the *Fear and Trembling* model, is joyful. Faith is certain and joy accompanies that certainty. In our elaboration of the *Fear and Trembling* model of faith, which goes beyond the presentation of faith by Johannes de Silentio without contradicting it, joy is the joy of faith given to us by God when He opens our eyes to the eternal goodness of His universe. It is not the product of our own wilful effort. It is the natural reaction to a realization and confident assurance of God's goodness shining through His creation.

10

Kierkegaard and Nietzsche

Kierkegaard and Nietzsche of course never met and never could have met: Nietzsche was a boy eleven years old growing up in Naumburg in the east of Germany when Kierkegaard died in his native Copenhagen in 1855. Nor did Nietzsche read Kierkegaard. By the end of Nietzsche's life, it is true, Kierkegaard was becoming known in Germany. In 1879 Georg Brandes published in German his *Literary Character-Sketch* on Kierkegaard.[1] Some years later, in 1888, the year before the onslaught of Nietzsche's madness, Brandes called the work of Kierkegaard to Nietzsche's attention, but it was too late for Nietzsche to acquire and read any of Kierkegaard's writings.[2]

In a dire and ironic symmetry, Kierkegaard and Nietzsche come to the end in the same way. Both literally collapsed in the street – Kierkegaard in Copenhagen in 1855, Nietzsche in Turin in 1889. Kierkegaard was taken to a hospital and died in a matter of weeks. Nietzsche was carried home and then taken by his friend Franz Overbeck to Basel. There he was taken to a clinic, and then to the asylum in Jena, though he was soon released to the care of his mother. After 1897 he lived under the care of his sister in Weimar, where he died in 1900. While Kierkegaard lived for only forty days after his collapse, Nietzsche lived for eleven years; his writing, however, ended in 1889. Kierkegaard died in 1855 at the age of 42; Nietzsche went insane in 1889 at the age of 44 and died in 1900 at the age of 55.

In much Kierkegaard and Nietzsche are alike. They are alike in their single-minded devotion to their work, their existential orientation, and their appreciation of the relevance of the psychological dimension of religion and morality. Finally, though, they are opposites; like mirror images they are profoundly similar and yet the reverse of one another in all significant particulars, so that finally they are absolutely opposed on what it means to live a human life at the fullest.

They are perhaps most clearly divided over religious belief in God. Undeniably this is a chief element of their opposition. However, the fault-line of their opposition regarding religious faith must be understood in order to understand the depth of their opposition. They are not opposed as are, say, William Paley, the champion of the teleological argument, and David Hume, the philosophical critic of that argument. The opposition between Paley and Hume is an intellectual opposition about the 'scientific' evidence for the proposition 'There is a God', said to be found in a design exhibited in the world and the probability provided by that evidence for that proposition.

Nor are Kierkegaard and Nietzsche opposed as are a traditional believer who confidently, if unreflectively, affirms the existence of God and an intellectual atheist (perhaps like Bertrand Russell) who upon reflection denies that there is a God. Theirs too is an intellectual opposition, precisely and completely about the truth of the proposition 'There is a God.' Nor are they opposed as John Calvin, the Protestant reformer who makes predestination theologically central to Christianity, and Voltaire, who rejects the 'superstition' of religious theism for a form of religious deism. Here the opposition is importantly over the conception of God and the importance of doctrine; this opposition is still essentially an intellectual opposition about the character of God and the status of doctrine – although Calvin's and Voltaire's opposing conceptions have implications for religious observance and attitude.

Nor are Kierkegaard and Nietzsche opposed quite as Alyosha and Ivan Karamazov are. Alyosha becomes a 'monk in the world', and Ivan, in reaction to the evil done to children, sends back his 'ticket' of admission to God and in this way, it has been said, defies God without denying God. Ivan is distanced from Alyosha by a great difference in passionate reaction, so that the opposition between the Karamazovs is far from merely intellectual (although Ivan would deny God's goodness – the truth of that proposition – and Alyosha would affirm it in faith). Whether or not Alyosha is a knight of faith (and it could be argued that his faith is that of a knight), he is very different from the philosophical and literary Kierkegaard. Ivan, again, is different from Nietzsche, for Ivan's 'rebellion' is not marked by an exuberant acceptance of 'the death of God'. It is rather, from Ivan's own perspective, a definite, chosen relationship to God, one of defiance.

Nor is the opposition between Kierkegaard and Nietzsche quite that between Naphta and Settembrini, even though the opposition between Thomas Mann's characters is as richly variegated as that between Kierkegaard and Nietzsche. Thomas Mann in his essays wrote about Nietzsche and in his fiction drew upon Nietzsche's life. In the 1940s Mann wrote *Doctor Faustus*, a novel which is his contribution to the body of literature inspired by the Faust legend. As we know, Mann modelled his Dr Faustus on Nietzsche. Mann's Faustus, like Nietzsche, lives for his 'work' (Mann makes his Faustus a driven composer); and, like Nietzsche, Faustus loses the light of his creativity to the darkness of syphilitic madness. It is earlier, in *The Magic Mountain*, that Mann gives us Settembrini and Naphta, who in many respects stand at opposite moral and spiritual poles. To the extent that they do, the opposition between Mann's characters is like the opposition between Kierkegaard and Nietzsche. But in Mann's rendering both Settembrini and Naphta in their complexity embody Nietzschean elements, for each echoes certain Nietzschean ideas and sensibilities. Yet Nietzsche is neither Settembrini nor Naphta. Nietzsche as much as Settembrini would be revolted by such religious excesses as kissing the sores of lepers, for which Naphta has something akin to nostalgia; but Nietzsche is opposed to Settembrini's faith in progress and his nearly slavish devotion to the ideals of the Enlightenment. Nor would he share Settembrini's humanistic appreciation of the dignity of man. Humankind, for Nietzsche, was still very far from becoming a 'bridge' to the *Übermensch*. True, when Settembrini renounces religion and its mystification, Nietzsche would agree. But while Nietzsche would judge Settembrini's absolute rejection of religious belief to be right, for Nietzsche Settembrini's rationalistic reasons for rejecting religion do not penetrate far enough. Nietzsche is, in many ways, closer to Naphta.

Naphta is the dark, religious figure, who opposes Settembrini, the apotheosis of utilitarian reason. It is Naphta who is aware of the deep psychological penetration of religious sensibilities, of the human dimension beyond reason and the rational avoidance of pain. It is Naphta who proclaims that religion has nothing to do with reason and morality. And it is Naphta who understands, as Nietzsche does, that religion cannot be pulled out of one's life without remaking the entire life. For both, rejecting religion is not merely a matter of proclaiming certain religious formulae to be false. However, Naphta embraces his dark image of religion, as

Nietzsche never would. Finally, then, Nietzsche is not Naphta, just as he is not Settembrini – and just as Kierkegaard is neither Naphta nor Settembrini.

Kierkegaard, like Nietzsche, would be opposed to Settembrini's encyclopedist sensibility that all that needs doing for human attainment is to bend our knowledge and technology to the elimination of pain. Kierkegaard, equally with Nietzsche, would be opposed to Naphta's sympathy for flagellation and scourge-loving asceticism, and he, perhaps more than Nietzsche, would reject Naphta's adulation of the warlike monks of the Middle Ages who shed blood unsparingly to establish the kingdom of God. Thus the opposition between Kierkegaard and Nietzsche is not the opposition between Settembrini and Naphta, for neither Kierkegaard nor Nietzsche is either Settembrini or Naphta.

While Kierkegaard and Nietzsche are opposed regarding religious faith, it is not too much to say that their opposition is uniquely their own. To fill it in we would need to rehearse the myriad aspects of the thought of each on faith, a matter to which we have devoted some chapters. Something similar could be said about their opposition regarding ethics.

Mann in his essay 'Nietzsche's Philosophy in the Light of Contemporary Events', written in the late 1940s, criticizes Nietzsche for separating ethics and life – for making life and morals opposites.[3] Mann's criticism, I would argue, at a minimum needs a strong qualification. Moreover, if this criticism can be levelled at Nietzsche, the same or a similar criticism may be applied to Kierkegaard in that he or Johannes de Silentio, in *Fear and Trembling*, separates ethics, the universal ethics$_1$, from the life of faith. Really, though, neither Kierkegaard nor Nietzsche sees morality as separated from a fully lived life. However, for each, the morality that fits a fully lived life is not conventional morality, which of course is not to say that Kierkegaard and Nietzsche agree about the character of the requisite non-conventional ethics.

Perhaps it would be useful, in thinking about the opposition between Kierkegaard and Nietzsche, to ask how they would have seen one another. How would Nietzsche have seen Kierkegaard? It would be hard for Nietzsche to see Kierkegaard's faith – as he presents it in *Fear and Trembling*, in the *Postscript*, or elsewhere in his authorship – as involving a secret desire for revenge. One with faith as Kierkegaard presents it, unlike the believers Nietzsche envisions, is not turning the other cheek to his enemies while harbouring a secret wish for revenge. This, of course, is not to say that Kierkegaard thought that his contemporaries had faith; rather, he challenged the habitual and social believers of Christendom to acknowledge the true demands of faith.

For Nietzsche, faith, in one theme-line in *The Antichrist*, is a doing. Faith for Johannes in *Fear and Trembling* is never precisely, and so only, a doing; yet the *expression* of Abraham's faith is a doing, an undertaking as much at odds with popular understanding as anything undertaken by Nietzsche or Zarathustra. So too Kierkegaard himself may have seen the expression of his faith as the calling – the doing – of his writing. (In fact, given what he tells us about his authorship in *The Point of View for my Work as an Author*, Kierkegaard did see his writing as being his special task in service to Christianity – about which more shortly.) To the extent that Kierkegaard was engaged in his *work*, and the *doing* of his faith, Nietzsche might well have had some sympathy for Kierkegaard; however, he would have had little sympathy for *what* Kierkegaard was doing – challenging those in Christendom to have faith and so to become Christians.

Might Nietzsche have seen Kierkegaard as being like the voluntary beggar, Nietzsche's Jesus-figure in *Thus Spoke Zarathustra*? The voluntary beggar, we will recall, is the giver of the sermon on the mound, who preaches to cows. Unlike the ugliest man, he is a doer. He has overcome nausea and he creates a new value, but the value he creates is passivity, 'chewing the cud'. And he is a plant-and-root man who denies the joys of the earth. Might Nietzsche have seen Kierkegaard as a doer, but as a creator of life-denying values? Kierkegaard hardly took the path of passivity: he challenged his society and in his last years he opposed himself to the established church in Denmark. Perhaps, though, Nietzsche might have seen Kierkegaard as wrongly oriented toward power and the will to power, for Kierkegaard did not recognize or seek to serve the value of power, as Nietzsche espoused. However, to his credit, from Nietzsche's perspective, Kierkegaard did not surreptitiously seek to aggrandize his own power by making others weak, as does the priestly type for Nietzsche.

Would Nietzsche have seen Kierkegaard as denying the joys of the earth? If Nietzsche were to have looked closely at Kierkegaard's

life or just at *Fear and Trembling* he would have found no endorse-
ment of asceticism. Kierkegaard sees monasticism with Protestant
eyes. In fact, he would seem to regard it more severely than does
his Lutheran heritage. For Kierkegaard, monasticism is a retreat
from the world into infinite resignation, while faith requires engagement in the world in such a way that not even the most
humble expression of the finite is irrelevant to faith. One might
recall here Johannes' portrayal of the contemporary knight of faith
walking home thinking of the dinner that will await him: he anticipates a delicacy, although it is all the same to him when his dinner
is standard fare.

In fact Nietzsche is more ascetic than Kierkegaard. Kierkegaard,
who inherited a small fortune from his father, had more than one
servant, enjoyed good food and wine, and rented elegant apart-
ments.[4] Nietzsche had no fortune and lived frugally; often ill and
regularly suffering from migraines, he had a constitution that
necessitated an ascetic way of life.

Taking another tack, perhaps Nietzsche would have seen
Kierkegaard as he saw Pascal. In *The Antichrist* Nietzsche says,
'Christianity ... has corrupted the reason even of those strongest in
spirit.... The most pitiful example: the corruption of Pascal, who
believed in the corruption of his reason through original sin when
it had in fact been corrupted by his Christianity.'[5] If Nietzsche had
made such a comment regarding Kierkegaard, he no doubt would
have accused Christianity of corrupting Kierkegaard's sensibility as
well as his reason.

Perhaps Nietzsche would have attributed to Kierkegaard and to
his religious belief the motive of weariness, which, as we noted in
Chapter 5, is the motive that Zarathustra sees for the creation of 'all
gods and afterworlds'. This weariness, says Zarathustra in a part of
the passage not quoted before, 'wants to reach the ultimate with
one leap, with one fatal leap'.[6] It is almost as though Nietzsche
were addressing Kierkegaard's category of the leap of faith, a category that is most often associated with the *Postscript* but is also
present in *Fear and Trembling*.[7]

Might Nietzsche also have seen Kierkegaard as too severely
denying the aesthetic? It is arguable that there was a profound
difference between Nietzsche and Kierkegaard on the aesthetic,
understanding the aesthetic as that orientation of life that empha-
sizes the immediate and the manipulation of the immediate. For
Nietzsche, Kierkegaard may have wrongly renounced – or

reduced – the aesthetic, first in favour of the ethical, as in *Either/Or*, and then in favour of the religious, as in *Fear and Trembling*. This disagreement signals what is finally one of the deepest divisions between Kierkegaard and Nietzsche, the division over the role of individual will. This is the division we found in the previous chapter, in its relation to the provenance of joy. To the cleft of this division and its larger implications we shall return, but now let us consider how Kierkegaard would have regarded Nietzsche.

How would Kierkegaard have seen Nietzsche? Close to the end of *Concluding Unscientific Postscript* Kierkegaard, or Johannes Climacus, allows that, in contrast to one inspired to propagate Christianity, who the busier he is propagating the more he shows he is not a Christian, there may be 'a scoffer [who] attacks Christianity and at the same time expounds it so creditably that it is a delight to read him, and the person who is really having a hard time getting it definitely presented almost has to resort to him.'[8] Kierkegaard in this passage, it has been suggested, is probably alluding to Ludwig Feuerbach, the author of *The Essence of Christianity*.[9] Robert Bretall in a note to this passage says that while Kierkegaard may have been thinking of Feuerbach, 'we can hardly help thinking of Nietzsche'.[10] Ultimately Kierkegaard must disagree with Nietzsche's understanding of Christianity, but, as I have suggested, he would have found in Nietzsche's psychological animadversions a challenge to what is deepest in Christianity and a challenge that he could not ignore.

How would Kierkegaard have seen Zarathustra's joyful acceptance of life/eternity? Kierkegaard might well have seen Zarathustra's acceptance as very like infinite resignation, for it is a matter of one's own willing effort. Moreover, Zarathustra's acceptance lacks the joy of faith, a joy that flows from a certainty that all manner of thing will be well. Though it has its own repose as a kind of acceptance, and though it has its own kind of joy, Zarathustra's acceptance, since it is not faith, is, for Kierkegaard, a species of despair.

Kierkegaard, under the pseudonym of Anti-Climacus, wrote an entire work on the typology and anatomy of despair. One of his categories in this work, *The Sickness unto Death*, is 'In Despair to

Will to be Oneself: Defiance'. Kierkegaard, or Anti-Climacus, says that when a person has this kind of despair:

> [t]he self is its own master, absolutely its own master, so-called; and precisely this is the despair, but also what it regards as its pleasure and delight.... In despair the self wants to enjoy the total satisfaction of making itself into itself, of developing itself, of being itself; it wants to have the honor of this poetic, masterly construction, the way it has understood itself.[11]

Gregor Malantschuk, who quotes this passage, argues that here 'with great accuracy a state of mind is portrayed which has a striking resemblance to Nietzsche's'.[12] Another passage that follows the one just quoted seems just as uncannily prescient; again it is almost as though Kierkegaard wrote it with Nietzsche in mind.

> The despairing person who in despair wills to be himself is unwilling to [hope in the possibility that an earthly need, a temporal cross, can come to an end]. He has convinced himself that this thorn in the flesh gnaws so deeply that he cannot abstract himself from it.... He is offended by it, or, more correctly, he takes it as an occasion to be offended at all existence.... [I]n spite of or in defiance of all existence, he wills to be himself with it [existence], takes it along, almost flouting his agony. Hope in the possibility of help, especially by virtue of the absurd, that for God everything is possible – no, that he does not want. And to seek help from someone else – no, not for all the world does he want that. Rather than to seek help, he prefers, if necessary, to be himself with all the agonies of hell.[13]

Nietzsche did indeed will to be himself, to create himself, his values and his own meaning. To seek help from God would have been worse than a failure for Nietzsche: it would have been false to all he stood for. And Nietzsche did strive to be his own master, to fill for himself the role that God had played for many. The madman in *The Gay Science* rhetorically asks, 'Must we ourselves not become gods simply to appear worthy of [our having killed God]?' For Nietzsche we must. As Camus says in *The Myth of Sisyphus*, 'for Nietzsche, to kill God is to become god oneself'.[14] Furthermore, the second passage from *The Sickness unto Death* surely captures how Kierkegaard would characterize Nietzsche's acceptance of existence as it is expressed in Zarathustra's Dionysian embrace of the agonies of life/eternity.

For Malantschuk, Nietzsche is among those 'who wish to remain in the sphere of the aesthetic', and for Kierkegaard, as Malantschuk sees, Nietzsche would be a demonic figure.[15] Anti-Climacus says of defiant despair, 'The more consciousness there is in such a sufferer who in despair wills to be himself, the more his despair intensifies and becomes demonic.'[16] The demonic in *Fear and Trembling*, we recall, is a highly realized form of the aesthetic, one in which the demoniac enters an absolute relationship to the demonic, that is, to his or her own resolution or will. Allowing Anti-Climacus and Johannes de Silentio to collaborate, we find projected a picture of Nietzsche as a demoniac, fully conscious of his defiance, who replaces God with his own resolution or will.

So, I suggest, Kierkegaard would see Nietzsche. But now there is an ironic twist. Walter Lowrie observes that the terms Kierkegaard uses to describe the despair of defiance are 'substantially equivalent' to those he uses to describe himself 'in the character of the "young friend" in the Second Part of *Either/Or*'.[17] The 'young friend' in *Either/Or* is the aesthetic author of *Either/Or*, Part I, who is known as A, and he is addressed as 'my young friend' by B, Judge William, who is – in the sense of 'ethical' that is found in *Either/Or* – the ethical author of the Second Part of *Either/Or*. Judge William addresses and admonishes A from his standpoint of the ethical. At one point he says this:

> you practice the art of being mysterious to everybody. My young friend, suppose there was no one who cared to guess your riddle – what joy would you have in it then? But above all for your own sake, for the sake of your salvation – for I know no condition of the soul that can better be described as damnation – halt this wild flight, this passion for annihilation that rages within you, for that is what you want: you want to annihilate everything; you want to satisfy the hunger of your doubt by consuming existence. For this you fashion yourself, and for this you toughen your mind.[18]

In 1847 Kierkegaard made entries in his journal that make it clear that 'he regarded his dissolute life and his defection from Christianity [in his youth] as due not essentially to doubt, but to despair and to rebellion against God'.[19]

Nor is this all. The one who in despair wills to be himself, Anti-Climacus says, has a 'thorn in the flesh'. Kierkegaard speaks of his own thorn in the flesh more than once, notably in a work that he wrote in 1848 under his own name, but which was not published in an unabridged form during his lifetime. That work is *The Point of View for My Work as an Author*, and in it Kierkegaard says: 'I had a thorn in the flesh, intellectual gifts (especially imagination and dialectic) and culture in superabundance, an enormous development as an observer, a Christian upbringing that was certainly very unusual, [and] a dialectical relationship to Christianity which was peculiarly my own....'[20] Kierkegaard's use of a 'thorn in the flesh' of course refers to Paul and his thorn in the flesh. The relevant passage is in Paul's second letter to the Corinthians. After receiving 'visions and revelations of the Lord' and 'being caught up to the third heaven' Paul says, 'to keep me from being too elated by the abundance of revelations, a thorn was given me in the flesh' (2 Cor. 12:1–2 and 7). In 1843, as we had occasion to note in Chapter 4, Kierkegaard published a collection of four discourses, *Four Upbuilding Discourses* (1843); in 1844 he published another set of four discourses, *Four Upbuilding Discourses* (1844) – non-pseudonymously, as he published all his discourses. One of these four is entitled 'The Thorn in the Flesh'. Of Paul's thorn in the flesh, Kierkegaard says the Apostle Paul 'knows that it is beneficial to him, and that this thorn in the flesh is given him so that he will not be arrogant.' 'The mark of the apostle', Kierkegaard continues, 'is that he does not become unsteady, which may happen even to the most honest person who experienced the blessedness of heaven, but who also, when the thorn began to pain and fester, knew of nothing but to moan.'[21] For Paul a thorn in the flesh is beneficial, but for one who is not an apostle a thorn in the flesh can gnaw and lead one in quite another direction. It can be the occasion of rebellion and defiance. Kierkegaard did not regard himself as an apostle and consistently denied that he spoke with authority.[22] Did he then regard his thorn in the flesh as the occasion for despair?

In 1848 Kierkegaard wrote of himself in his journal, 'From the earliest time I have winced at a thorn in the flesh, to which also a consciousness of sin and guilt associated itself. I have felt myself heterogeneous. This pain, this heterogeneousness of mine, I have understood as my God-relationship.'[23] In 1852 he wrote in his journal, 'Understanding myself to be fundamentally different from others, also with a thorn in the flesh, I became an author in great inner suffering.'[24] For Kierkegaard, in his own self-understanding, he was, as he tells us in *The Point of View*, 'a religious author from the beginning'.[25] However, we also find in the journals this:

> There are some purely human lives in which religion comes first. They are those who from the beginning have suffered and are cut off from the universal by some particular suffering, to whom the enjoyment of life is denied and who therefore must either become purely demoniacal – or else essentially religious.[26]

Kierkegaard in his own eyes was a religious author in a special relation to Christianity, with a special calling as a religious author to address in his authorship 'the problem of becoming a Christian in Christendom'.[27] But at the same time, he appreciated, his thorn in the flesh could tempt him to the demonic, for, as in *Fear and Trembling*, the religious and the demonic, though utter opposites, are alike in being ways open to those 'cut off from the universal'.

If Lowrie is right and Kierkegaard in *The Sickness unto Death* is describing himself when he describes the despairing person who in despair wills to be himself, then in one final irony, Kierkegaard as well as Nietzsche may have suffered from this form of despair, or at least found it a beckoning temptation. The difference of course is that Nietzsche would not recognize his despair, or would embrace it as healthy, while Kierkegaard, to the extent that he felt this form of despair or its appeal, would recognize and confess it with sorrow. In any event, to the extent Kierkegaard experienced in himself a proclivity toward defiant despair he would have had, not pity, but a natural sympathy for Nietzsche.

In general the opposition that divides Kierkegaard and Nietzsche is mainly religious and moral, although this does not deny that it has an intellectual dimension. It certainly has cognitive implications that relate to religion and morality. Within this opposition a signal difference, a deep-reaching cleft, is over the place of will, the will of the individual in human resolution as the means to fulfilment. For Kierkegaard in *Fear and Trembling*, while the exercise of one's will is sufficient for infinite resignation, it is not sufficient for faith, and, moreover, in both *Fear and Trembling* and *The Sickness unto Death*, complete reliance upon and devotion to one's own will, to one's own resolution, is demonic. For Nietzsche, as we have seen, it is by one's own will that one creates value and meaning – and it is will that wrenches one into joy.

Let us be clear on the geography of this dividing chasm regarding the will. If we think of Kierkegaard as the author of all his pseudonymous and non-pseudonymous works, this chasm, strictly, does not divide Kierkegaard and Nietzsche. It does, however, divide the Kierkegaard of *Fear and Trembling* and Nietzsche, especially as Nietzsche is expressed by his *alter ego*, Zarathustra, for faith in *Fear and Trembling* is decidedly not a matter of one's own will.

Other models of faith are closer to Nietzsche in giving a great place to will and in either giving no place to joy or in not seeing what we discover – what it is given to us to know – as the source of joy. One such model is in fact provided by Kierkegaard himself through the pseudonymous author Johannes Climacus. For Climacus in the *Postscript*, as I observed in Chapter 1, faith is a continuing struggle to overcome one's doubts and to hold fast in belief an 'objective uncertainty'. Faith, for Climacus, is a matter of will in that it is the passion that results from the continuing struggle to believe an uncertainty. Climacus is clear that faith and knowledge exclude one another: if we know to be true what is to be accepted on faith, faith is impossible, on the *Postscript* model of faith. This means that whatever joy there is in faith on this model does not derive from religious knowledge, as it does on the *Fear and Trembling* model.

Not surprisingly, when Climacus shows us a portrait of a contemporary religious individual in accord with the *Postscript* model, the joyfulness of his faith is not in evidence.[28] Climacus' religious individual knows that he can act only through God and can do nothing of himself. The frailest expression of the finite is implicated in his God-relationship. In these aspects of his religious sensibility he is not so different from the contemporary, or any, knight of faith, the exemplar of the model of faith found in *Fear and Trembling*. The religious individual of the *Postscript*, in what Climacus gives us, would go to the Deer Park, a large wooded park north of Copenhagen that included an amusement park. But unlike the comfortable believers of Christendom, who go to the Deer Park without a second thought, the religious individual has a question that he must face. Is it allowable for him to go to the Deer Park? It is ethically allowable, but is it religiously allowable? Does his God-relationship allow it? Is this a diversion he needs, a needed rest from the requirements of his God-relationship, or is it a 'fancy of immediacy'?[29] He is not sure; indeed he is suffused with doubt, so much so that he is in a 'crisis of sickness', although Climacus assures us that 'this sickness is not unto death'.[30] That is, it is not despair. As his faith is a struggle to believe in the face of doubt, so he has to struggle with doubt to decide whether he may do such a thing as go on an outing at the Deer Park. Finally he resolves to go in the face of his unresolved doubts, and he does go. Once there he enjoys himself, Climacus says.[31] The contrast with Johannes de Silentio's contemporary knight of faith is evident. The contemporary knight does not struggle to determine the requirements of his God-relationship. He exhibits a seeming insouciance in his daily round which is more in accord with the joyfulness at the centre of his faith.

Miguel de Unamuno gives us another model of faith that makes will central to faith. Apparently inspired by Kierkegaard's *Postscript*, Unamuno gives us a model of faith that is close to the model provided by Johannes Climacus, but is in one significant respect different. For Unamuno, true faith suffers in unovercome doubt; yet its very strength is born from its struggle with the 'gimlet of doubt'.[32] With Unamuno's model of faith believers do not have faith; yet they try with every fibre to believe, and so affirm the faith they do not have. If the cry of faith for the *Postscript* model is 'It cannot be, all reason is against it; yet I believe!' the cry of faith for Unamuno's model is 'I cannot believe; God have mercy upon me!' For the *Postscript* model believers believe by overcoming their doubt and uncertainty by an act of will. They choose to believe, and do believe in the face of their own doubts and in the face of no evidence and even negative evidence against there being a God. They strive to believe, and succeed in doing so. For Unamuno's model of faith, believers strive to believe but do not succeed. Their faith is their striving. Unamuno's story, 'Saint Manuel Bueno, Martyr', has as its protagonist such a believer. At any rate, the story and Don Manuel are open to this construction. Don Manuel is the priest in a small Spanish village, Valverde de Lucerna. He is well loved by those in the village and known as a saintly man. Yet, while he helps others to believe, he himself cannot believe. He falls silent when he reaches the last verse of the Creed, although this is unnoticed in the village. He trembles when he gives Communion, but this too is unnoticed. Because his life is selfless, his secret – that he cannot believe – goes undetected. Don Manuel chooses to believe, and tries to believe, but cannot. His faith is his effort of will to believe. Here indeed is a model of faith that gives a place to will. And what place is there for joy in this model of faith? For Unamuno faith is far from passionless, but its defining passion is agony. For him faith is steeped in agony; it is 'agonic'. He writes, 'Our Spanish crosses, our Spanish Christs are terribly tragic: they represent the worship of Christ in agony, not yet dead…. [I]t is this Christ, the Christ of "My God, my God, why hast thou forsaken me?" (Matt. 27:46), that agonic believers worship.'[33] And for Unamuno, as this Christ expresses kenotic doubt, so religious worship, if it is to reflect true faith, is not free of the agony of doubt. The passion of faith is not joy on Unamuno's model, but agony, the agony of doubt and the endless struggle against doubt.[34]

So far as the role of will goes (though not on other matters), there is no deep opposition between these two models of faith and Nietzsche's thinking. But where faith is faith on the *Fear and Trembling* model – and this model is in accord with a deeply-woven strand in more than one tradition of religious belief – there is a deep cleft between Kierkegaard and Nietzsche on the role of will. This opposition over the will is an opposition for our age. At the end of the twentieth century the secularization of our sensibilities is no longer a distinctly Western phenomenon. Across cultures the traditional religions are losing their capacity to speak to our post-modern hearts and minds. For the wraith of Nietzsche, we need a new madman with a new message: all the gods are dying. Their moribund shadows may yet flicker on the walls of our cultural caves, but their substance is gone. Very different are the intuitions of a Kierkegaard applied to the age: we continue to turn from God, but now we do so with a frank audacity, suppressing our sense of the transcendent and closing off to ourselves what alone can fulfil us, an entered relationship to the Divine. In this way the opposition between Kierkegaard and Nietzsche over the role of will speaks to us in our emerging multicultural and postmodern world with a new and pressing relevance that perhaps neither could have foreseen from their vantage points in the nineteenth century. Do we choose the way of will or the way of faith? Or – expanding the choice to include religions that do not make faith central – do we choose the way of will or the way of religious commitment to the transcendent? Or is it that our choosing must be given to us?

Notes

Introduction

1. Friedrich Nietzsche, *Twilight of the Idols*, in *The Portable Nietzsche*, ed. and trans. Walter Kaufmann (New York: Viking Press, 1954), p. 549.
2. At the very end of *Thus Spoke Zarathustra* Zarathustra asks, 'Am I concerned with *happiness* [*Glücke*]?' and replies, 'I am concerned with my *work* [*meinem Werke*]', in *The Portable Nietzsche*, p. 439. Henceforth cited as Nietzsche, *Thus Spoke Zarathustra*.
3. Friedrich Nietzsche, *Ecce Homo*, '*Thus Spake Zarathustra*: A Book for all and None', Sec. 1, in *The Philosophy of Nietzsche* (New York: The Modern Library, 1954), p. 894. Cited by Henry David Aiken, 'An Introduction to *Zarathustra*', in *Nietzsche: A Collection of Critical Essays*, ed. Robert C. Solomon (Garden City, New York: Anchor Press/Doubleday, 1973), p. 114.
4. *Übermensch* is usually translated as 'overman'; however, *Mensch* means 'human being' and so a better translation might be 'overbeing' or 'overindividual'. Since 'overman' can be misleading and the other translations are unfamiliar I shall use the German *Übermensch* untranslated.
5. Friedrich Nietzsche, *The Antichrist*, in *The Portable Nietzsche*, p. 625. Henceforth cited as Nietzsche, *The Antichrist*.
6. Nietzsche, *Thus Spoke Zarathustra*, First Part, 'On the Afterworldly', p. 143.
7. *The Cognitivity of Religion: Three Perspectives* (London: Macmillan; Berkeley and Los Angeles: University of California Press, 1985), chapter 2, pp. 91–133.

1 Abraham, the Knight of Faith

1. Søren Kierkegaard, *Concluding Unscientific Postscript to* Philosophical Fragments, vol. 1, ed. and trans. Howard V. and Edna H. Hong (Princeton: Princeton University Press, 1992), p. 244. Henceforth cited as Kierkegaard, *Postscript*.
2. Ibid., p. 186.
3. Ibid., p. 557.
4. Ibid., p. 686.
5. Ibid., pp. 203–4.
6. All references to the Bible are to the Revised Standard Version. For a discussion of these two models of faith, and of a third related model, see my 'Three Models of Faith', *International Journal for Philosophy of Religion*, vol. 12 (1981); reprinted in *Contemporary Perspectives on Religious Epistemology*, ed. R. Douglas Geivett and Brendan Sweetman (New York, Oxford: Oxford University Press, 1992). We shall have occasion to note the third model in Chapter 10.

7. Søren Kierkegaard, *Fear and Trembling* with *Repetition*, ed. and trans. Howard V. and Edna H. Hong (Princeton: Princeton University Press, 1983), p. 3; and see the note on p. 339. Henceforth cited as Kierkegaard, *Fear and Trembling*.

8. Kierkegaard's source for the Abraham story is the Bible. The story of Abraham's trial of faith, and his being called upon to sacrifice his son, is also found in the Koran (37.99–106). In the Islamic tradition the son is Ismael, not Isaac (the son is not named in the Koranic passage). The Koranic story otherwise is in essence the same.

9. Kierkegaard, *Fear and Trembling*, p. 20.

10. Johannes de Silentio's retelling is contained in the 'Eulogy on Abraham' and the 'Preliminary Expectoration', *Fear and Trembling*, pp. 15–23 and 27–53.

11. Kierkegaard, *Fear and Trembling*, p. 18.

12. Ibid., p. 22.

13. Ibid., p. 35.

14. Ibid., p. 20.

15. Ibid., p. 36.

16. Ibid., p. 20.

17. Ibid., p. 36.

18. Ibid., p. 36.

19. Ibid., p. 40.

20. Ibid., p. 28. The Danish word that Hong and Hong translate as 'anxiety' is *Angst* (old form: *Angest*). Others translate *Angst* as 'dread'. Walter Lowrie in his earlier translation of *Fear and Trembling*, and in his translation of *Begrebet Angest* as *The Concept of Dread*, used the alternative translation. I shall use both English words.

21. Kierkegaard, *Fear and Trembling*, p. 30.

22. Kierkegaard, *The Concept of Anxiety*, ed. and trans. Reidar Thomte in collaboration with Albert B. Anderson (Princeton: Princeton University Press, 1980), p. 61. Henceforth cited as Kierkegaard, *The Concept of Anxiety*.

23. Ibid., p. 91.

24. Ibid., pp. 46 ff, 56, 80 ff.

25. Ibid., p. 117.

26. Kierkegaard, *Fear and Trembling*, pp. 55–6.

27. Ibid., pp. 10–14.

28. Ibid., p. 40.

29. Ibid., p. 55.

30. Ibid., p. 23.

31. Ibid., p. 50.

2 The Joyfulness of Faith

1. Kierkegaard, *Fear and Trembling*, p. 22.

2. Kierkegaard, *Postscript*, p. 211. Climacus says that what one knows, or as good as knows, one cannot believe; what is known cannot be the object of faith. (*Tro* in Danish translates as either 'belief' or 'faith'.)

3. Jean-Paul Sartre, *L'Existentialisme est un humanisme*, published in English as *Existentialism*, trans. Bernard Frectman (New York: Philosophical Library, 1947), pp. 22–3; Frectman's translation is reprinted in part as 'Existentialism' in *Existentialism and Human Emotions* (New York: Philosophical Library, 1985), p. 19.
4. Sartre, *Existentialism*, p. 23; 'Existentialism', *Existentialism and Human Emotions*, p. 20.
5. Jean-Paul Sartre, *Being and Nothingness*, trans. Hazel E. Barnes (New York: Philosophical Library, 1956), p. 29.
6. Kierkegaard, *Fear and Trembling*, pp. 113 and 115.
7. Ibid., p. 71.
8. Ibid., pp. 82 ff.
9. Ibid., p. 31.
10. For more on the contrast between Charles Manson and Abraham, as he is presented in *Fear and Trembling*, see Gene Outka, 'Religious and Moral Duty: Notes on *Fear and Trembling*', *Religion and Morality*, ed. Gene Outka and John P. Reeder, Jr (Garden City, New York: Anchor Press/Doubleday, 1973), pp. 229–30, and my *God-Relationships With and Without God* (London: Macmillan; New York: St. Martin's, 1989), pp. 28–9 and 30–1.

3 The Ethical, Infinite Resignation, and the Demonic

1. Kierkegaard, *Fear and Trembling*, p. 54.
2. Ibid., p. 82.
3. Ibid., pp. 57–9.
4. Ibid., p. 54.
5. Ibid., p. 60.
6. Martin Buber, *Eclipse of God* (New York and Evanston: Harper & Row, 1957), pp. 117–18.
7. Ibid., p. 118.
8. Ibid., p. 115.
9. Milton Steinberg, 'Kierkegaard and Judaism', *Anatomy of Faith* (New York: Harcourt Brace, 1960), p. 147 (Steinberg's emphasis). Quoted by Louis Jacobs, 'The Problem of the *Akedah* in Jewish Thought', *Kierkegaard's* Fear and Trembling: *Critical Appraisals*, ed. Robert L. Perkins (Alabama: The University of Alabama Press, 1981), p. 3.
10. Jacobs, 'The Problem of the *Akedah* in Jewish Thought', pp. 1–2.
11. Buber, *Eclipse of God*, p. 118.
12. Jacobs, 'The Problem of the *Akedah* in Jewish Thought', pp. 8–9.
13. Kierkegaard, *Fear and Trembling*, p. 70.
14. Ibid., p. 66.
15. Ibid., p. 74.
16. For a related discussion of Kierkegaard's implicit distinction between the ethical$_1$ and the ethical$_2$, see my *God-Relationships With and Without God*, pp. 20–7.
17. Kierkegaard, *Fear and Trembling*, p. 65.

18. Ibid., p. 33 (emphasis in text). Johannes, however, does sometimes use 'hero' or the expression 'hero of faith' in connection with knights of faith. See pp. 15 and 51. It remains that the tragic hero, and not the knight of faith, is a hero in the straightforward sense that he, or she, receives the acclaim and admiration of many.
19. Ibid., p. 45.
20. Ibid., p. 34.
21. Ibid., p. 40.
22. Ibid., p. 38.
23. Ibid., p. 36.
24. Ibid., p. 37.
25. Ibid., pp. 40–1.
26. Ibid., p. 46.
27. Ibid., pp. 49–50.
28. Ibid., p. 18.
29. Ibid., pp. 41–5.
30. Ibid., p. 41n.
31. Ibid., p. 40.
32. Ibid., p. 48.
33. Ibid., p. 49.
34. Cf. Robert Merrihew Adams, 'The Knight of Faith', *Faith and Philosophy*, vol. 7 (1990), pp. 391–2. Adams believes that, for Johannes, infinite resignation, and so faith as well, requires 'concentration of desire on a single finite object'. While Johannes sometimes suggests that infinite resignation requires a 'concentration of desire on a single finite object', given the instance of the contemporary knight of faith, this cannot be quite right – unless 'everything' is 'a single finite object'. Adams also suggests that there are three movements of faith in *Fear and Trembling*, the first being the movement of 'the concentration of desire on a single finite object'. This point can be right only if what is infinitely resigned always *is* 'a single finite object'.
35. Kierkegaard, *Fear and Trembling*, p. 48.
36. Ibid., p. 49.
37. Ibid., p. 49.
38. Ibid., p. 48.
39. Ibid., p. 44.
40. Ibid., p. 35.
41. Ibid., p. 45.
42. Ibid., p. 34.
43. Adams, 'The Knight of Faith', p. 389.
44. Kierkegaard, *Fear and Trembling*, p. 50.
45. Ibid., p. 35.
46. *Either/Or* is a pseudonymous work 'edited' by Victor Eremita. It was published in 1843, the same year *Fear and Trembling* was published, though *Either/Or* was published first. 'The Seducer's Diary' is written by a pseudonymous contributor identified in *Either/Or* only as 'Johannes'. Later, in *Stages on Life's Way* and in *Concluding Unscientific Postscript*, he will be referred to as Johannes the Seducer; he is not, of course, to be confused with Johannes de Silentio. Søren Kierkegaard,

Either/Or, I, ed. and trans. Howard V. and Edna H. Hong (Princeton: Princeton University Press, 1987), pp. 301–445.

47.　Kierkegaard, *Fear and Trembling*, pp. 89–92.
48.　Ibid., pp. 94–7.
49.　Ibid., p. 96.
50.　Ibid., p. 97.
51.　Ibid., p. 110.
52.　Ibid., p. 109.
53.　Another demonic figure who does good, mentioned by Johannes, is 'Cumberland's Jew' (p. 106). In Richard Cumberland's play *The Jew* the central figure, Scheva, is widely regarded as a miser and usurer, while in fact he does great good works, though in secret. This play was presented in Kierkegaard's Copenhagen many times. See Hong and Hong's n. 43 on p. 354 and Walter Lowrie's corresponding note to his translation of *Fear and Trembling*, in *Fear and Trembling and The Sickness unto Death*, trans. Walter Lowrie (Princeton: Princeton University Press, 1941), pp. 269–70, n. 83.
54.　Kierkegaard, *Fear and Trembling*, p. 96.
55.　Ibid., p. 105.
56.　Ibid., p. 107n.
57.　Ibid., p. 97.
58.　However, *after* he has entered the demonic he will need God's help to return to the ethical – and so it will not be merely a matter of his choosing at that point, but will require a 'movement by virtue of the absurd', Johannes says (pp. 98–9).
59.　Kierkegaard, *Fear and Trembling*, pp. 112–13.

4　Knights of Faith

1.　Kierkegaard, *Fear and Trembling*, p. 38.
2.　Ibid., p. 28.
3.　Ibid., p. 38.
4.　Ibid., pp. 38–41.
5.　Ibid., pp. 40–1.
6.　For Kierkegaard, the contemporary knight of faith 'belongs to this world' in several senses: first, he is in outward demeanour very like his fellows in the world; second, he does not have the monastic spirituality of the Middle Ages, which renounces 'the world' ('to enter a monastery is not the highest', says Johannes de Silentio, *Fear and Trembling*, p. 100); and, third, the contemporary knight of faith believes for this world, as opposed to focusing belief on a reward in a future life. Abraham, too, belongs to the world in these senses, we should observe: he belongs to the world in the first sense before his trial of faith, and he belongs to the world in the second and third senses both before and after his trial. Neither Abraham's belonging to the world nor that of the contemporary knight of faith, then, comes to Abraham or the contemporary knight of faith as being 'worldly' with that kind of worldliness – being attached to

the things of this world – that alienates one from God and tends to or is sin.

7. Elisha returns with the Shunammite woman to her home, where her dead son lies, and, through Elisha's prayers, her son is returned to life (2 Kings 4:32–7). As Abraham does not lose Isaac, so the Shunammite woman does not lose her son. However, this does not mean that 'all will be well', as it relates to the contemporary knight of faith and other knights of faith, entails that in no case will a knight's child be lost to him or her.

8. Julian of Norwich, chapter 13 of *Showings* (Short text); *Julian of Norwich: Showings*, ed. and trans. Edmund Colledge and James Walsh (New York: Paulist Press, 1978), p. 149.

9. We may, in other words, attribute to the contemporary knight of faith what I have elsewhere called a realization-discovery of God's presence. See my *The Cognitivity of Religion: Three Perspectives* (London: Macmillan; Berkeley and Los Angeles: University of California Press, 1985), pp. 104–11.

10. Kierkegaard, *Fear and Trembling*, p. 82.

11. Kierkegaard, *Postscript*, p. 505.

12. Ibid., pp. 246–7.

13. Søren Kierkegaard, 'The Lord Gave and the Lord Took Away; Blessed Be the Name of the Lord', *Four Upbuilding Discourses* (1843), in *Eighteen Upbuilding Discourses*, ed. and trans. Howard V. Hong and Edna H. Hong (Princeton: Princeton University Press, 1990), p. 122.

14. Søren Kierkegaard, *Fear and Trembling* with *Repetition*, pp. 198–9. Henceforth cited as Kierkegaard, *Repetition*. It is not that the Young Man was rejected. Rather the Young Man broke off the relationship. Constantin Constantinius in Part I tells us that the Young Man 'left in the lurch' the girl who is the cause of his misery: 'One day he did not show up and sent no word at all' (p. 181).

15. Kierkegaard, *Repetition*, p. 198.

16. Ibid., p. 204.

17. Ibid., p. 205.

18. Ibid., p. 207.

19. Ibid., p. 209.

20. Ibid., p. 210.

21. Ibid., p. 229.

22. This selection from Kierkegaard's papers and journals is in the Supplement provided by Hong and Hong in *Fear and Trembling* with *Repetition*, p. 328.

23. However, cf. Hong and Hong's n. 44 on p. 372 of *Fear and Trembling* with *Repetition*, in which they say: 'All of them [knights of faith and heroes of faith] represent positions beyond that of Job.' Their note is to the Young Man's comment that 'Job does not bring composure as does a hero of faith', which was quoted above. To be sure, the Young Man does not see Job as a hero (or knight) of faith, but for the reasons I have given we need not follow him in this.

24. Kierkegaard, *Fear and Trembling*, pp. 64–5.

25. Ibid., pp. 102–4.

26.   Ibid., p. 104.
27.   Johannes de Silentio is clear that knights of faith are not heroes in this latter sense, as we saw in Chapter 3. See also n. 18 to Chapter 3.

5   Nietzsche as the Antichrist

1.   So Walter Kaufmann tells us in his introduction to *The Antichrist*, *The Portable Nietzsche*, p. 565.
2.   Gary Shapiro, 'The Writing on the Wall: *The Antichrist* and the Semiotics of History', *Reading Nietzsche*, ed. Robert C. Solomon and Kathleen M. Higgens (New York: Oxford University Press, 1988), pp. 212–13. It is not accidental that the title of Walter Kaufmann's book on Nietzsche is *Nietzsche: Philosopher, Psychologist, Antichrist* (fourth edition; Princeton: Princeton University Press, 1974).
3.   Shapiro, 'The Writing on the Wall: *The Antichrist* and the Semiotics of History', p. 212.
4.   Friedrich Nietzsche, *The Antichrist*, p. 589 (emphasis in the text).
5.   Ibid., p. 589 (emphasis in the text).
6.   Ibid., p. 575.
7.   Ibid., pp. 590–1 (emphasis in the text).
8.   Ibid., p. 576 (emphasis in the text).
9.   Ibid., p. 571.
10.   Ibid., p. 570.
11.   Friedrich Nietzsche, *Beyond Good and Evil*, Part 9, 'What is Noble', *The Philosophy of Nietzsche* (New York: Modern Library, 1954), pp. 579–80. Henceforth cited as Nietzsche, *Beyond Good and Evil*.
12.   Nietzsche, *The Antichrist*, pp. 593–4 (emphasis in the text).
13.   Ibid., pp. 611–12.
14.   Ibid., p. 597 (emphasis in the text).
15.   Ibid., p. 618.
16.   'The Attack upon "Christendom"', *A Kierkegaard Anthology*, ed. Robert Bretall (Princeton: Princeton University Press, 1946), pp. 439–41.
17.   Nietzsche, *The Antichrist*, p. 631.
18.   Ibid., p. 571.
19.   Ibid., p. 634.
20.   Ibid., pp. 572–3 (emphasis in the text).
21.   Friedrich Nietzsche, *Thus Spoke Zarathustra*, p. 143.
22.   Nietzsche, *The Antichrist*, p. 602 (emphasis in the text).
23.   Ibid., p. 613.
24.   Ibid., pp. 624–5 (emphasis in the text). The passage from Paul is 1 Cor. 1:27–9.
25.   Nietzsche, *The Antichrist*, p. 623 (emphasis in the text). The relevant passage in Sec. 10 of the First Essay in *The Genealogy of Morals* is in *The Portable Nietzsche*, p. 451. Kaufmann uses the French 'ressentiment', instead of the English 'resentment' because Nietzsche used the French word and because 'resentment' does not capture Nietzsche's conception. See Kaufmann, *Nietzsche: Philosopher, Psychologist, Antichrist*, pp. 371–8 for Kaufmann on 'ressentiment'.
26.   Nietzsche, *The Antichrist*, p. 605 (emphasis in the text).

27. Ibid., p. 608 (emphasis in the text).
28. Ibid., pp. 606–7 (emphasis in the text).
29. Ibid., pp. 612–13 (emphasis in the text).
30. Ibid., p. 609 (emphasis in the text).
31. Ibid., p. 607 (emphasis in the text).
32. Ibid., p. 601. See also p. 603. By the time Nietzsche wrote *The Antichrist* he had discovered Dostoyevsky's *The Idiot*. See Kaufmann's note, *The Antichrist*, p. 601; and see Kaufmann's *Nietzsche: Philosopher, Psychologist, Antichrist*, p. 340 and p. 340, n. 2, for the extent of Nietzsche's acquaintance with Dostoyevsky's novels.
33. Nietzsche, *Thus Spoke Zarathustra*, p. 381 (emphasis in the text).
34. Ibid., p. 382. The section in *Thus Spoke Zarathustra* that is entitled 'The Voluntary Beggar', in which the voluntary beggar is presented, is pp. 380–4. The quotations that follow are from these pages.

6 Zarathustra, the Prophet of the *Übermensch*, and the Death-of-God Theme

1. Kaufmann, 'Editor's Preface' to *Thus Spoke Zarathustra*, *The Portable Nietzsche*, p. 103.
2. Nietzsche, *Thus Spoke Zarathustra*, p. 124 (emphasis deleted).
3. Ibid., p. 128.
4. Ibid., pp. 135 and 136.
5. Ibid., pp. 122–4 (emphasis in the text).
6. Emil L. Fackenheim, *The Religious Dimension in Hegel's Thought* (Boston: Beacon Press, 1967), p. 210.
7. Kaufmann, *Nietzsche: Philosopher, Psychologist, Antichrist*, p. 100, n. 3.
8. Owen Chadwick, *The Secularization of the European Mind in the Nineteenth Century* (Cambridge: Cambridge University Press, 1975), pp. 218–19.
9. Algernon Charles Swinburne, 'Hymn of Man', II. 176 and 198.
10. Friedrich Nietzsche, *The Gay Science*, trans. Walter Kaufmann (New York: Random House, 1974), Aphorism 125, pp. 181–2 (emphasis in the text).
11. Ibid., Aphorism 343, p. 279.
12. Nietzsche, *Thus Spoke Zarathustra*, 'Retired', pp. 370–5. The following quotations are from these pages.
13. Ibid., p. 202.
14. Ibid., p. 373.
15. Ibid., p. 294.
16. Ibid., 'The Ugliest Man', pp. 375–9.
17. Ibid., p. 376 (emphasis in the text).
18. Ibid., p. 426 (emphasis deleted).
19. Nietzsche, *The Gay Science*, Aphorism 108, p. 167.
20. Nietzsche, *Thus Spoke Zarathustra*, p. 191 (emphasis deleted).
21. Ibid., p. 199.
22. Ibid., p. 292.
23. Ibid., p. 197.
24. Ibid., p. 197.

7 Transvaluation

1. Nietzsche, *Thus Spoke Zarathustra*, p. 308.
2. Nietzsche, *The Antichrist*, p. 577 (emphasis in the text).
3. Nietzsche, *Beyond Good and Evil*, p. 378 (emphasis in the text).
4. Fyodor Dostoyevsky, *The Brothers Karamazov*, trans. David Magarshack (Harmondsworth and Baltimore: Penguin Books, 1958), I, pp. 77–8 and 309.
5. Ibid., I, pp. 308–9.
6. Albert Camus, *The Rebel*, trans. Anthony Bower (New York: Random House, 1956), p. 71. Though Camus is reflecting on 'God's death', his exact formulation is: 'if nothing is true, everything is permitted', in Ivan Karamazov's thinking; and 'if nothing is true, nothing is permitted', in Nietzsche's 'profounder logic'.
7. Nietzsche, *The Antichrist*, p. 577.
8. Nietzsche, *Thus Spoke Zarathustra*, p. 188.
9. Ibid., pp. 400–3.
10. Ibid., pp. 399–403 (emphasis in the text).
11. Nietzsche, *Beyond Good and Evil*, pp. 579–81.
12. Nietzsche, *Thus Spoke Zarathustra*, p. 302.
13. Ibid., p. 583; and *The Antichrist*, p. 589.
14. Nietzsche, *Thus Spoke Zarathustra*, p. 226.
15. Robert C. Solomon, 'Nietzsche, Nihilism, and Morality', in *Nietzsche: A Collection of Critical Essays* (Garden City, New York: Anchor Press/Doubleday, 1973), p. 224 (Solomon's emphasis).
16. Nietzsche, *Thus Spoke Zarathustra*, p. 187.
17. Ibid., p. 202 (emphasis in the text).
18. Ibid., p. 228.
19. Cf. Mary Warnock, *Existentialist Ethics* (London: Macmillan; New York: St. Martin's, 1967), pp. 47–8 and 56.
20. Søren Kierkegaard, *Works of Love*, trans. Howard and Edna Hong (New York: Harper & Row, 1962).

8 Eternal Recurrence and Joyful Acceptance

1. Nietzsche, *Thus Spoke Zarathustra*, 'On the Vision and the Riddle', pp. 271–2 (emphasis deleted).
2. Ibid., 'The Convalescent', pp. 328–31.
3. Ibid., pp. 269–70 (emphasis in the text).
4. Nietzsche, *The Gay Science*, Aphorism 341, pp. 273–4 (emphasis in the text).
5. Kaufmann, *Nietzsche: Philosopher, Psychologist, Antichrist*, pp. 317–19, and cf. Kaufmann's Translator's Introduction to *The Gay Science*, pp. 15–17.
6. Quoted by Kaufmann in *Nietzsche: Philosopher, Psychologist, Antichrist*, p. 318 and in his Translator's Introduction to *The Gay Science*, p. 16.
7. Nietzsche, *Thus Spoke Zarathustra*, p. 269 (emphasis in the text).

8. Friedrich Nietzsche, *The Birth of Tragedy*, in *The Birth of Tragedy and The Case of Wagner*, trans. Walter Kaufmann (New York: Random House, 1967), p. 60 (emphasis in the text). Henceforth cited as Nietzsche, *The Birth of Tragedy*.

9. Nietzsche, *The Birth of Tragedy*, p. 42.

10. Henry A. Fischel, 'The Transformation of Wisdom in the World of Midrash', in *Aspects of Wisdom in Judaism and Early Christianity*, ed. Robert L. Wilkin (Notre Dame and London: University of Notre Dame Press, 1975), pp. 84–6 and 98, n. 94.

11. Ibid., p. 98, n. 95. See Plutarch's *Moralia* 115 b–e for the Aristotelian fragment from *Eudemas* or *On the Soul*; this passage in the *Moralia* is in *Select Fragments*, vol. 12 of *The Works of Aristotle*, ed. W. D. Ross (Oxford: Clarendon Press, 1952), pp. 18–19.

12. Arthur Schopenhauer, *The World as Will and Representation*, trans. E. F. J. Payne (New York: Dover, 1966), vol. II, pp. 585–8.

13. Nietzsche, *Thus Spoke Zarathustra*, p. 245.

14. Friedrich Nietzsche, *Twilight of the Idols*, in *The Portable Nietzsche*, p. 473 (emphasis in the text).

15. Nietzsche, *Thus Spoke Zarathustra*, pp. 430 and 439.

16. Ibid., p. 434.

17. Ibid., pp. 336–9.

18. Ibid., pp. 340–3.

19. Albert Camus, *The Myth of Sisyphus*, in *The Myth of Sisyphus and Other Essays*, trans. Justin O'Brien (New York: Random House, 1960), p. 90. Henceforth cited as Camus, *The Myth of Sisyphus*.

20. Ibid., p. 91.

21. Nietzsche, *Thus Spoke Zarathustra*, 'The Dancing Song', pp. 219–22.

22. Ibid., 'The Other Dancing Song', pp. 336–8.

23. Ibid., pp. 338–40.

24. Nietzsche, *Thus Spoke Zarathustra*, 'The Seven Seals (Or: The Yes and Amen Song)', pp. 340–3.

25. Kaufmann does so in his Editor's Notes on 'The Other Dancing Song', *The Portable Nietzsche*, p. 263.

26. Nietzsche, *Thus Spoke Zarathustra*, 'The Drunken Song', pp. 429–30.

27. Ibid., pp. 430–6.

28. Ibid., p. 436 (emphasis in the text).

29. Ibid., p. 432.

30. Nietzsche, *The Birth of Tragedy*, p. 60 (emphasis in the text).

31. Nietzsche was aware of the Dionysian aspect of Zarathustra's acceptance of life and eternity, his 'everlasting Yea to all things'. See *Ecce Homo*, '*Thus Spake Zarathustra*: A Book for All and None', Secs. 6 and 7; in *The Philosophy of Nietzsche*, pp. 902 and 903.

9   The Joy of Faith and the Joy of Zarathustra's Acceptance

1. Kierkegaard, *Fear and Trembling*, p. 69.

2. Nietzsche, *The Antichrist*, p. 613 (emphasis deleted).

3. Kierkegaard, *Fear and Trembling*, pp. 122–3.

4. *Conversations with Nietzsche: A Life in the Words of His Contemporaries*, ed. Sander L. Gillman, trans. David J. Parent (New York and Oxford: Oxford University Press, 1987), p. 109.

5. Nietzsche, *Thus Spoke Zarathustra*, p. 383.

6. Ibid., pp. 380–1.

7. Ibid., p. 439 (emphasis in the text).

8. Aldous Huxley, *The Doors of Perception* (New York: Harper & Row, 1954), pp. 64–5.

9. Kierkegaard, *Fear and Trembling*, pp. 49–50.

10. Ibid., p. 41.

11. Johannes mentions it twice in the 'Eulogy on Abraham'. Kierkegaard, *Fear and Trembling*, pp. 17 and 19.

12. See *The Cognitivity of Religion*, pp. 112–17, for different settings for the kind of religious discovery embodied in the Psalmist's experience; and see above, Chapter 4, n. 9.

13. See *The Cognitivity of Religion*, pp. 117–30, esp. p. 120, for a discussion of the issue between the tradition of the Psalms and Nietzsche over such a discovery-experience, or realization-discovery, of God and His goodness.

10   Kierkegaard and Nietzsche

1. Walter Lowrie, *Kierkegaard*, vol. 1 (New York: Harper & Brothers, 1962), p. 3.

2. Kaufmann, *Nietzsche: Philosopher, Psychologist, Antichrist*, p. 125.

3. Thomas Mann, 'Nietzsche's Philosophy in the Light of Contemporary Events', in Solomon, *Nietzsche: A Collection of Critical Essays*, p. 368.

4. Walter Lowrie, *Kierkegaard*, vol. 2 (New York: Harper & Brothers, 1962), pp. 502–3; and Patrick Gardiner, *Kierkegaard* (Oxford and New York: Oxford University Press, 1988), p. 12.

5. Nietzsche, *The Antichrist*, pp. 571–2; Gregor Malantschuk suggests that Nietzsche might have seen Kierkegaard this way in his 'Kierkegaard and Nietzsche', in *A Kierkegaard Critique*, ed. Howard A. Johnson and Niels Thulstrup (Chicago: Henry Regnery, 1962), p. 126.

6. Nietzsche, *Thus Spoke Zarathustra*, p. 143.

7. Kaufmann thinks that this passage in *Thus Spoke Zarathustra* contains what would have been Nietzsche's reaction to Kierkegaard: *Nietzsche: Philosopher, Psychologist, Antichrist*, p. 125.

8. Kierkegaard, *Postscript*, p. 614.

9. Søren Kierkegaard, *Concluding Unscientific Postscript to Philosophical Fragments*, vol. 2, ed. and trans. Howard V. and Edna H. Hong (Princeton: Princeton University Press, 1992), p. 270, n. 862; and Søren Kierkegaard, *Concluding Unscientific Postscript*, trans. David F. Swenson and Walter Lowrie (Princeton: Princeton University Press, 1941), p. 573, n. 8.

10. Robert Bretall (ed.), *A Kierkegaard Anthology* (Princeton: Princeton University Press, 1946), p. 257, n. 2.
11. Søren Kierkegaard, *The Sickness unto Death*, ed. and trans. Howard V. and Edna H. Hong (Princeton: Princeton University Press, 1980), p. 69. Henceforth cited as Kierkegaard, *The Sickness unto Death*.
12. Malantschuk, 'Kierkegaard and Nietzsche', p. 125. Malantschuk quotes a bit more than I have, and in a slightly different translation.
13. Kierkegaard, *The Sickness unto Death*, pp. 70–1.
14. Camus, *The Myth of Sisyphus*, p. 80. Camus says this in a passage on Kirilov, Dostoyevsky's character in *The Possessed*, who commits suicide to assert against God his own freedom and will. The full quotation is: 'For Kirilov, as for Nietzsche, to kill God is to become god oneself; it is to realize on this earth the eternal life of which the Gospel speaks.'
15. Malantschuk, 'Kierkegaard and Nietzsche', pp. 124 and 125.
16. Kierkegaard, *The Sickness unto Death*, pp. 71–2.
17. Lowrie makes this observation in a note to his translation of *The Sickness unto Death*, in *Fear and Trembling* and *The Sickness unto Death*, p. 275, n. 21. Hong and Hong similarly refer to *Either/Or*, II in a note to their translation. Kierkegaard, *The Sickness unto Death*, p. 177, n. 69.
18. Søren Kierkegaard, *Either/Or*, II, ed. and trans. Howard V. and Edna H. Hong (Princeton: Princeton University Press, 1987), p. 160.
19. Lowrie, *Kierkegaard*, vol. 1, p. 187.
20. Søren Kierkegaard, *The Point of View for My Work as an Author*, trans. Walter Lowrie, ed. Benjamin Nelson (New York: Harper & Brothers, 1962), p. 82. Henceforth cited as Kierkegaard, *The Point of View*. This passage in a slightly different translation is quoted by Lowrie in *Kierkegaard*, vol. 1, p. 50. Lowrie in *Fear and Trembling* and *The Sickness unto Death* draws to our attention the fact that 'thorn in the flesh' had a special significance for Kierkegaard: p. 275, n. 22; and Hong and Hong in a note to this phrase in their translation refer to *The Point of View*. Kierkegaard, *The Sickness unto Death*, p. 177, n. 70.
21. Søren Kierkegaard, 'The Thorn in the Flesh', *Four Upbuilding Discourses* (1844), in *Eighteen Upbuilding Discourses*, p. 329.
22. See, for instance, Kierkegaard's prefaces to his several collections of upbuilding discourses, including his preface to *Four Upbuilding Discourses* (1844), in *Eighteen Upbuilding Discourses*, p. 295.
23. Quoted by Lowrie, *Kierkegaard*, vol. 2, p. 404.
24. Alexander Dru, ed. and trans., *The Journals of Kierkegaard* (New York and Evanston: Harper & Row, 1958), p. 215.
25. Kierkegaard, *The Point of View*, p. 13.
26. Bretall, *A Kierkegaard Anthology*, p. 323.
27. Kierkegaard, *The Point of View*, p. 92.
28. Kierkegaard, *Postscript*, pp. 472–97.
29. Ibid., p. 495.
30. Ibid., p. 488.
31. Ibid., p. 493.

32. Miguel de Unamuno, 'What is Truth?', in *The Agony of Christianity and Essays on Faith*, trans. Anthony Kerrigan (Princeton: Princeton University Press, 1974), p. 175.
33. Unamuno, 'Agony', in *The Agony of Christianity and Essays on Faith*, p. 10.
34. Much of this paragraph I have adopted from my 'Three Models of Faith'.

Bibliography

1. R. M. Adams, 'The Knight of Faith', *Faith and Philosophy*, vol. 7 (1990).
2. H. D. Aiken, 'An Introduction to *Zarathustra*', in Solomon (61).
3. R. Bretall (ed.), *A Kierkegaard Anthology* (Princeton: Princeton University Press, 1946).
4. M. Buber, *Eclipse of God* (New York and Evanston: Harper & Row, 1957).
5. A. Camus, *The Myth of Sisyphus*, in Camus (6).
6. A. Camus, *The Myth of Sisyphus and Other Essays*, trans. Justin O'Brien (New York: Random House, 1960).
7. A. Camus, *The Rebel*, trans. Anthony Bower (New York: Random House, 1956).
8. O. Chadwick, *The Secularization of the European Mind in the Nineteenth Century* (Cambridge: Cambridge University Press, 1975).
9. F. Dostoyevsky, *The Brothers Karamazov*, 2 vols, trans. David Magarshack (Harmondsworth and Baltimore: Penguin Books, 1958).
10. A. Dru (ed. and trans.), *The Journals of Kierkegaard* (New York and Evanston: Harper & Row, 1958).
11. E. L. Fackenheim, *The Religious Dimension in Hegel's Thought* (Boston: Beacon Press, 1967).
12. H. A. Fischel, 'The Transformation of Wisdom in the World of Midrash', in Wilkin (70).
13. P. Gardiner, *Kierkegaard* (Oxford and New York: Oxford University Press, 1988).
14. R. D. Geivett and B. Sweetman (eds), *Contemporary Perspectives on Religious Epistemology* (New York and Oxford: Oxford University Press, 1992).
15. S. L. Gillman (ed.), *Conversations with Nietzsche: A Life in the Words of His Contemporaries*, trans. David J. Parent (New York and Oxford: Oxford University Press, 1987).
16. A. Huxley, *The Doors of Perception* (New York: Harper & Row, 1954).
17. L. Jacobs, 'The Problem of the *Akedah* in Jewish Thought', in Perkins (54).
18. H. A. Johnson and Niels Thulstrup (eds), *A Kierkegaard Critique* (Chicago: Henry Regnery, 1962).
19. Julian of Norwich, *Julian of Norwich: Showings*, ed. and trans. Edmund Colledge and James Walsh (New York: Paulist Press, 1978).
20. W. Kaufmann, *Nietzsche: Philosopher, Psychologist, Antichrist* (fourth edition; Princeton: Princeton University Press, 1974).
21. W. Kaufmann (ed. and trans.), *The Portable Nietzsche* (New York: Viking Press, 1954).
22. J. Kellenberger, *The Cognitivity of Religion: Three Perspectives* (London: Macmillan; Berkeley and Los Angeles: University of California Press, 1985).

23. J. Kellenberger, *God-Relationships With and Without God* (London: Macmillan; New York: St. Martin's, 1989).
24. J. Kellenberger, 'Three Models of Faith', *International Journal for Philosophy of Religion*, vol. 12 (1981); reprinted in Geivett and Sweetman (14).
25. S. Kierkegaard, 'The Attack upon "Christendom"', in Bretall (3).
26. S. Kierkegaard, *The Concept of Anxiety*, ed. and trans. Reidar Thomte in collaboration with Albert B. Anderson (Princeton: Princeton University Press, 1980).
27. S. Kierkegaard, *Concluding Unscientific Postscript*, trans. David F. Swenson and Walter Lowrie (Princeton: Princeton University Press, 1941).
28. S. Kierkegaard, *Concluding Unscientific Postscript to* Philosophical Fragments, 2 vols, ed. and trans. Howard V. and Edna H. Hong (Princeton: Princeton University Press, 1992).
29. S. Kierkegaard, *Eighteen Upbuilding Discourses*, ed. and trans. Howard V. Hong and Edna H. Hong (Princeton: Princeton University Press, 1990).
30. S. Kierkegaard, *Either/Or*, 2 vols, ed. and trans. Howard V. and Edna H. Hong (Princeton: Princeton University Press, 1987).
31. S. Kierkegaard, *Fear and Trembling*, in Kierkegaard (32).
32. S. Kierkegaard, *Fear and Trembling* with *Repetition*, ed. and trans. Howard V. and Edna H. Hong (Princeton: Princeton University Press, 1983).
33. S. Kierkegaard, *Fear and Trembling* and *The Sickness unto Death*, trans. Walter Lowrie (Princeton: Princeton University Press, 1941).
34. S. Kierkegaard, 'The Lord Gave and the Lord Took Away; Blessed Be the Name of the Lord', *Four Upbuilding Discourses* (1843), in Kierkegaard (29).
35. S. Kierkegaard, *The Point of View for My Work as an Author*, trans. Walter Lowrie, ed. Benjamin Nelson (New York: Harper & Brothers, 1962).
36. S. Kierkegaard, *Repetition*, in Kierkegaard (32).
37. S. Kierkegaard, *The Sickness unto Death*, ed. and trans. Howard V. and Edna H. Hong (Princeton: Princeton University Press, 1980).
38. S. Kierkegaard, 'The Thorn in the Flesh', *Four Upbuilding Discourses* (1844), in Kierkegaard (29).
39. S. Kierkegaard, *Works of Love*, trans. Howard and Edna Hong (New York: Harper & Row, 1962).
40. W. Lowrie, *Kierkegaard*, 2 vols (New York: Harper & Brothers, 1962).
41. G. Malantschuk, 'Kierkegaard and Nietzsche', in Johnson and Thulstrup (18).
42. T. Mann, 'Nietzsche's Philosophy in the Light of Contemporary Events', in Solomon (61).
43. F. Nietzsche, *The Antichrist*, in Kaufmann (21).
44. F. Nietzsche, *Beyond Good and Evil*, in Nietzsche (49).
45. F. Nietzsche, *The Birth of Tragedy*, in Nietzsche (46).
46. F. Nietzsche, *The Birth of Tragedy and The Case of Wagner*, trans. Walter Kaufmann (New York: Random House, 1967).

47. F. Nietzsche, *Ecce Homo*, in Nietzsche (49).
48. F. Nietzsche, *The Gay Science*, trans. Walter Kaufmann (New York: Random House, 1974).
49. F. Nietzsche, *The Philosophy of Nietzsche* (New York: The Modern Library, 1954).
50. F. Nietzsche, *Thus Spoke Zarathustra*, in Kaufmann (21).
51. F. Nietzsche, *Twilight of the Idols*, in Kaufmann (21).
52. G. Outka, 'Religious and Moral Duty: Notes on *Fear and Trembling*', in Outka and Reeder (53).
53. G. Outka and J. P. Reeder, Jr (eds), *Religion and Morality* (Garden City, New York: Anchor Press/Doubleday, 1973).
54. R. L. Perkins (ed.), *Kierkegaard's* Fear and Trembling: *Critical Appraisals* (Alabama: The University of Alabama Press, 1981).
55. W. D. Ross (ed.), *Select Fragments*, vol. 12 of *The Works of Aristotle* (Oxford: Clarendon Press, 1952).
56. J.-P. Sartre, *Being and Nothingness*, trans. Hazel E. Barnes (New York: Philosophical Library, 1956).
57. J.-P. Sartre, *L'Existentialisme est un humanisme*, published in English as *Existentialism*, trans. Bernard Frectman (New York: Philosophical Library, 1947).
58. J.-P. Sartre, *Existentialism and Human Emotions* (New York: Philosophical Library, 1985).
59. A. Schopenhauer, *The World as Will and Representation*, 2 vols, trans. E. F. J. Payne (New York: Dover, 1966).
60. G. Shapiro, 'The Writing on the Wall: *The Antichrist* and the Semiotics of History', in Solomon and Higgens (63).
61. R. C. Solomon (ed.), *Nietzsche: A Collection of Critical Essays* (Garden City, New York: Anchor Press/Doubleday, 1973).
62. R. C. Solomon, 'Nietzsche, Nihilism, and Morality', in Solomon (61).
63. R. C. Solomon and K. M. Higgens (eds), *Reading Nietzsche* (New York: Oxford University Press, 1988).
64. M. Steinberg, *Anatomy of Faith* (New York: Harcourt Brace, 1960).
65. M. Steinberg, 'Kierkegaard and Judaism', in Steinberg (64).
66. M. de Unamuno, 'Agony', in Unamuno (67).
67. M. de Unamuno, *The Agony of Christianity and Essays on Faith*, trans. Anthony Kerrigan (Princeton: Princeton University Press, 1974).
68. M. de Unamuno, 'What is Truth?', in Unamuno (67).
69. M. Warnock, *Existentialist Ethics* (London: Macmillan; New York: St. Martin's, 1967).
70. R. L. Wilkin (ed.), *Aspects of Wisdom in Judaism and Early Christianity* (Notre Dame and London: University of Notre Dame Press, 1975).

Index